Taming the

RICHARD JACKMAN and K

1. Indexation means that contracts for future payments would be expressed in terms of money of 'constant purchasing power'.

2. Such contracts would protect both parties against the effects of changes in the value of money, which may otherwise bring about redistributions of income and wealth. Thus indexation would eliminate some effects of inflation generally regarded as most undesirable.

3. Although much less harmful with indexation than without it, continued inflation would still be costly and largely pointless.

4. Despite popular belief to the contrary, it would be easier to slow down inflation with indexation than without it.

5. The widespread introduction of indexation need pose no insuperable transitional difficulties. It is not clear why trade unions should be against indexation.

6. Indexation of wages would be a much better way of achieving the aims now sought by 'incomes policy'. There may even be arguments for compulsory indexation.

7. Contrary to popular belief, indexation would not make it more difficult for the government to pursue policies of 'retrenchment'.

8. Indexation would cause difficulties if it were based on the Index of Retail Prices. A more appropriate index—the index of 'total home costs'—is therefore recommended.

9. If a particular exchange-rate régime is possible without indexation, it is also possible with indexation.

10. If governments are unwilling to index their own transactions and encourage indexation in the private sector, their declarations that they wish to protect citizens against the effects of inflation cannot be taken seriously.

Hobart Paper 63 is published (price £1.00) by

THE INSTITUTE OF ECONOMIC AFFAIRS
2 Lord North Street, Westminster
London SWIP 3LB   Telephone: 01-799 3745

IEA PUBLICATIONS

Subscription Service

An annual subscription to the IEA ensures that all regular publications are sent without further charge immediately on publication—representing a substantial saving.

The cost (including postage) is £10·00 for twelve months (£9·50 if by Banker's Order)—£7·50 for teachers and students; US $30 or equivalent for overseas subscriptions.

To: The Treasurer,
    Institute of Economic Affairs,
    2 Lord North Street,
    Westminster,
    London SW1P 3LB

Please register a subscription of £10·00 (£7·50 for teachers and bona fide students) for the twelve months beginning..............

☐ Remittance enclosed   ☐ Please send invoice

☐ I should prefer to pay by Banker's Order which reduces the subscription to £9·50.

Name ....

Address ....

        ....

Position ....

Signed..

Date...

Taming the Tiger

*An essay in the economic theory and
political economy of indexation
to mitigate the consequences of,
and slow down, inflation*

RICHARD JACKMAN

*Lecturer in Economics
London School of Economics*

KURT KLAPPHOLZ

*Reader in Economics
London School of Economics*

Published by
THE INSTITUTE OF ECONOMIC AFFAIRS
1975

First published September 1975

©

THE INSTITUTE OF ECONOMIC AFFAIRS 1975

All rights reserved

SBN 255 36073–8

Printed in Great Britain by
GORON PRO-PRINT CO LTD,
6 Marlborough Road, Churchill Industrial Estate, Lancing, Sussex

Text set in 'Monotype' Baskerville

The *Hobart Papers* are intended to contribute a stream of authoritative, independent and lucid analysis to the understanding and application of economics to private and government activity. Their characteristic concern has been with the optimum use of scarce resources and the extent to which it can be achieved in markets within an appropriate legal/institutional framework or by more effective arrangements.

One of the institutions that is commonly supposed to be a creation of government is a monetary system to facilitate buying and selling, lending and borrowing, saving and investing. The recent breakdown of the British currency in the Great Inflation since 1969-70 is the occasion for this *Hobart Paper* by Messrs Richard Jackman and Kurt Klappholz of the London School of Economics. It has long been a subject of debate among economists whether and how far the monetary mechanism can be left to government or should be taken out of its control in an automatic or semi-automatic system. During the 19th century the monetary mechanism of the Western industrialised countries was to a larger or lesser degree based on gold, which minimised the control of government over the supply and value of money. After the breakdown of the gold standard in 1931 there was increasing support among economists for systems of (government-) 'managed' money, and since the war for 'managed' international systems. Since the late 1960s, the evident failure of government, national and international, to 'manage' the monetary systems of the West with the object of avoiding the excesses of deflation and inflation has again turned the minds of economists and others to automatic or semi-automatic monetary systems.

The most automatic system is based on gold. The case for gold is again being made not so much because it lacks defects but because the alternative, control of money by government, would seem to have even more. Here a notable study by Mr William Rees-Mogg, the Editor of *The Times*, may indicate a change in informed and authoritative opinion in Britain: he argued that down the centuries prices linked to gold were impressively steady.[1] In making the contrary case against

---

[1] *The Reigning Error: The Crisis of World Inflation*, Hamish Hamilton, London, 1974: '. . . during the whole of this period [1661 to 1913] the British price system beat like a steady pulse, affected by economic and political events but with a strong natural tendency to return to normality' (p. 71).

gold,[1] Professor Milton Friedman of Chicago maintained that in 19th-century America and Britain gold brought neither a stable value of the currency nor stable economic conditions. In the UK the price level rose from 117 to 194 between 1789 and 1800, fell from 134 to 74 between 1873 and 1896, and rose from 74 to 103 between 1896 and 1912. He observed that the record was 'very far from the kind of perfect stability of prices' that the advocates of gold or the gold standard appeared to suppose. That may be a valid count against the *advocates* of gold who claim too much rather than against gold. The 19th-century record contrasts sharply with the record of paper currencies, and especially with the acceleration in the rate of inflation (and its obverse, the deterioration in the value of money) in the British economy in the last five years. The annual changes in average prices in the periods indicated by Professor Friedman are of the order of 2-3 to 5 per cent a *year*. Since 1970 the British paper currency has collapsed at a rate never before experienced in peace-time. In 1974 and so far in 1975 prices in Britain have been rising, and the value of money deteriorating, by 2 to 3 per cent per *month*. Until recently the expectation was that the annual rate of inflation would rise from around 20 per cent in 1974 and around 25 per cent in 1975 to 30 per cent or more in 1976. It now seems that the rate of inflation will decline towards the end of 1975. But the unprecedented peace-time inflation of the 1970s, especially since sterling was floated, is much more violent than the fluctuations in the price level in the 19th century. The 1970s' inflation is based on paper (and debt) multiplied by government, not on gold mined by profit-seeking prospectors and adding tiny amounts to the stock of gold.

The debate among economists between the two broad controls of the supply and value of money, which may be crudely epitomised as the choice between 'gold' and 'government', is therefore likely to continue. With his customary clarity and incisiveness, Professor Friedman put the alternatives rather differently: he argued the two methods of disciplining government were by gold, which he rejected, or by 'a mechanical rule to which they are required to adhere'—the rule by which they would 'increase the quantity of money by 5 per cent per year every year, day in and day out—week in, week out'. Ideally he would prefer a wholly automatic system without

[1] At a Conference of the International Monetary Market of the Chicago Mercantile Exchange, reprinted in *Reason*, June 1975.

government discretion but, since the machinery of monetary management was in being in the Federal Reserve System, he offered his 'mechanical' rule as the best 'less extensive reform' that was politically possible.[1] In their recent study on welfare economics, Professors C. K. Rowley and A. T. Peacock went even further in a more legalistic formula: the only solution to the control of inflation was 'a monetary constitution, which *eliminates* governmental control over the money supply in favour of non-discretionary expansion at rates that reflect the underlying rate of real growth of the economy'.[2] (Our italics.) To the objection of advocates of automatic systems that government could not be trusted to control the monetary system at all, Professor Friedman replied:

'If governments are so irresponsible in their monetary policy that paper money becomes completely unreliable and is eliminated, I find it hard to believe that the governments themselves will exist or that you will have a kind of world in which it will be possible for people to dream of trading on the basis of gold.'

Until the debate between 'government' and 'gold' is resolved, Britain more than any other Western country has to endure a monetary mechanism that post-war Conservative and Labour governments have failed to make inflation-proof. In these circumstances economists are turning their minds to methods of minimising the damage done by inflation. If inflation is politically endemic, are its consequences remediable or controllable? One such method was discussed by Professor Friedman in IEA Occasional Paper 41 in 1974 under the title *Monetary Correction*. In this *Hobart Paper* Richard Jackman and Kurt Klappholz take the discussion further by analysing the economic theory of indexation and discussing its application

---

[1] A more technical objection has been raised by Professor F. A. Hayek (in *Full Employment at Any Price?*, Occasional Paper 45, IEA, 1975): since there is no 'sharp distinction . . . in the real world . . . between what is to be regarded as money and what is not', it is difficult to prescribe the amount of money to be added to the amount in circulation. 'Some discretion' would therefore have to be left to government to ensure the convertibility of near-money into real money to avoid liquidity crises. But he agreed with Friedman that more or less automatic systems were the objective for normal times, although not made invariable by law. It would seem the choice of evils is occasional crises or venal government fatally tempted to inflate unless restrained by an outside control.

[2] *Welfare Economics: A Liberal Restatement*, Martin Robertson, London, 1975, p. 190.

to the British economy as it has developed in the unprecedented inflation that began towards the end of 1969. They discuss indexation as a method, not only of reducing or removing the consequences of inflation, but also of decelerating and mastering it.

The discussion of the economics of indexation is not new in economic writing. It goes back to at least the 1820s following the inflation during and after the Napoleonic wars. Among the participants have been some of the great names in economics: W. Stanley Jevons, Walter Bagehot, Robert Giffen, Alfred Marshall and J. M. Keynes. But they did not face the relatively frenetic inflation of the 1970s in which the British currency unit has lost approaching half its value in five years. This *Hobart Paper* is therefore all the more timely and in the grand tradition of British economics.

The authors' analysis is tightly argued. It will require close attention that will be worth the effort since it breaks new ground by grappling with the scope for indexation in government compacts and private contracts and with the possible opposition to it. In spite of the difficulty and novelty of the subject, the argument is presented as clearly as its nature permits, and it is amply illustrated by examples showing how indexation might be applied both in the government sector to taxes, borrowing and payments and in the private sector to savings, pay and prices. The authors also do not flinch from the complications of the transition from unindexed to indexed contracts. In all, they have written a model of economic analysis which economists and students of economics will find enlightening and stimulating and which non-economists will find it profitable to study, if necessary with a second or third reading.

Perhaps the central issue the authors discuss is the extent to which indexation could be left to develop spontaneously in the private sector (as it has done in building contract escalator clauses, etc.), or should be encouraged or compelled by government. On the ground that the effects of private transactions are not confined to the parties to them, so that there are 'external' effects on third parties, they argue three grounds for government encouragement or compulsion of indexed contracts in the private sector. The first is in capital markets: if borrowers and lenders differ in their expectations of the rate of inflation, unindexed lending may continue which would mis-allocate investment funds. What remains unclear is how far and how soon increasing experience may discourage people from entering into unindexed contracts so that indexed debts gradually replace them.

Second, there is an arguable case for compulsory indexation of wages, otherwise firms may make mistaken estimates of the rate of inflation, which would lead to bankruptcies and unemployment that government would be under pressure to prevent by inflationary monetary policy, as we in Britain have seen since 1971 with far-reaching consequences. Since the costs of these mistakes are shifted to third parties, there is a case for making the indexing of wages compulsory so that incorrect estimates of the future rate of inflation are avoided. This case for compulsion rests on the assumption that government would try to prevent bankruptcies and unemployment; the question is how long this can be done.

Third, if parties to a contract expect different rates of inflation, unindexed contracts can be used by individuals, companies or government itself to improve their position. The authors instance trade union leaders who expect a faster rate of inflation than do trade union members, so that they will be seen to achieve larger increases in real wages in times of inflation than in times of price stability and thus strengthen their position *vis à vis* their members; compulsory indexation would remove the scope for such gains by trade union leaders (who would therefore oppose it).

These three conditions, the authors argue, may provide a circumstantial case for government to encourage or compel indexation in private contracts. In general, of course, 'externalities' constitute a necessary but not a sufficient case for government interventions. How far they provide a conclusive case will depend on three further considerations: first, the financial and political cost of government encouragement or compulsion; second, the ability of government to improve on the rate at which individuals learn from experience and replace unindexed by indexed contracts spontaneously; third, the capacity of government to do what theory indicates they could do to accelerate the process of learning from experience rather than submit to the day-to-day pressures from capital or labour, buyers or sellers, lenders or borrowers, to which they will be exposed in devising forms of encouragement or compulsion. It would seem that the historical experience of government in its control of paper currencies does not strengthen the expectation that it will resist these pressures if, by submitting to them, it serves its objective of remaining in office or power.

In raising these and the other issues in their *Hobart Paper*, Messrs Jackman and Klappholz have written a penetrating, thoughtful and stimulating analysis that makes a contribution to the discussion, not only of indexation as the means of limiting or preventing the undesirable consequences of inflation, but also of the sources of inflation itself and how it may be avoided. They are sceptical of the view that indexation would accelerate inflation, particularly when based on the argument that trade unions are capable of causing continued inflation by 'excessive' wage claims. They maintain that indexation would ease the economic difficulty of slowing down the rate of inflation and therefore lessen the political obstacles. By contrast with either conventional deflationary or incomes policies, indexation combined with a slowing down in the rate of expansion of the money supply would create fewer distortions in relative prices, including wages. Not least interesting is their emphasis that even compulsory indexation does not comprise a 'wages policy' since it leaves relative prices free to move and so to perform their function of allocating capital, labour and other resources to the multiplicity of industries and occupations that contend for them.

The Institute is indebted to Professors Milton Friedman and Michael Parkin for reading a draft of the *Paper*. The constitution of the Institute requires it to dissociate the Trustees, Directors and Advisers from its authors' analyses and conclusions, but it commends this *Hobart Paper* to economists, students of economics and to non-economists in industry and government and in the communications media as an original contribution to a debate in Britain that will require resolution as long as government exercises power over the mechanism of money.

August 1975   ARTHUR SELDON

CONTENTS

		Page
PREFACE	*Arthur Seldon*	3
THE AUTHORS		11
ACKNOWLEDGEMENTS		11
I INTRODUCTION		13
Indexation reproduces correct expectations, not price stability		13
Indexation and the economy: some questions		14
II INDEXATION AND ECONOMIC WELFARE		15
Redistribution		15
Reduction of uncertainty		17
Efficiency		18
A. Anticipated inflation		19
B. Unanticipated inflation		19
III INDEXATION AND THE PROCESS OF INFLATION		23
(i) Inflation and tax revenue		23
(ii) The containment of inflation		25
(iii) 'Cost-push' inflation		27
Is indexation a form of incomes policy?		30
The 'dilemma'		30
(iv) The expectations theory of inflation		31
IV INDEXATION AND SPECIFIC CONTRACTS		35
The tax system		35
Government debt		37
National savings		40
Commercial debt		40
Banks		41
Building societies		41
Pension funds		42
Wages and salaries		42

V FOUR KEY ASPECTS   43

   The transition   43

   The choice of index   46
    'Value of money' index   46
    Index of 'total home costs'   46
    Index of retail prices   47

   Partial indexation   49

   Is there a case for compulsory indexation?   50
    (i) Indexation and capital markets   51
    (ii) Indexation to neutralise inflationary
       expectations   52
    (iii) Indexation and money illusion   52

VI INDEXATION, POLITICS AND ECONOMIC POLICY   53
    (i) Would the inflation rate continue to fluctuate
      in the absence of indexation?   54
    (ii) With indexation, would inflation matter?   55
    (iii) Indexation and the behaviour of the price level   56
    (iv) Indexation and some current issues of policy   57
   CONCLUSION   61

QUESTIONS FOR DISCUSSION   63

BIBLIOGRAPHY   64

THE AUTHORS

RICHARD JACKMAN was born in 1945 and educated at St. Paul's School and Churchill College, Cambridge, where he graduated in 1967. Since 1968 he has been a Lecturer in Economics at the London School of Economics.

His publications include 'Keynes and Leijonhufvud' (*Oxford Economic Papers*, July 1974), 'University Efficiency and University Finance' (with Richard Layard, published in *Essays in Modern Economics*, edited by Michael Parkin, 1973), 'The Problem of Externalities in a Spatial Economy' (in *Regional Science—New Concepts and Old Problems*, edited by E. L. Cripps, 1975), and a number of essays on local government finance. He has been a consultant to the London Boroughs' Association.

KURT KLAPPHOLZ is Reader in Economics at the London School of Economics. He was born in Bielsko (Silesia), Poland in 1927 and came to Britain in 1945. In 1947 he entered the London School of Economics and obtained a B.Sc.(Econ.) with First Class Honours in 1951. In 1951-2 he was a graduate assistant at Duke University, Durham, North Carolina, and from 1952-54 he was an Instructor in Economics at Columbia University, New York. In 1954 he was appointed to the staff of LSE.

He has had articles published on the methodology of economics and on the theory of economic policy in *The Economic Journal*, *The British Journal for the Philosophy of Science*, *Economica*, and elsewhere.

ACKNOWLEDGEMENTS

We are indebted to many people, at the LSE and elsewhere, for comments on drafts, and in particular to Brian Hindley and Morris Perlman for a careful analysis of our argument and many helpful suggestions.

R.J.
K.K.

July 1975

I. INTRODUCTION

The purpose of this *Hobart Paper* is to examine the case for indexation or 'monetary correction' in the light of economic theory. But an important part of the argument is concerned with the effect of indexation on government economic policy, which necessarily involves political as well as economic considerations. The *Paper* is self-contained but may be regarded as complementary to Professor Milton Friedman's *Monetary Correction*,[1] in which the theoretical arguments for indexation are largely taken as read.

With indexation, contracts for future payment would be denominated not simply in terms of money, but in money of constant purchasing power. If the value of money were to change after the signing of a contract, its monetary value would change by the same proportion. The real value of such contracts would therefore be independent of, and hence protected against, changes in the value of money.

Indexation reproduces correct expectations, not price stability

It is sometimes suggested that indexation would create a situation equivalent to that in which 'the value of money were again stable'.[2] This is not strictly correct. Indexation creates a situation in which the real value of contracts is not disturbed by changes in the price level after signing the contract. Thus it is more closely equivalent to a situation in which future changes in the price level are correctly foreseen by everyone. In practice, price stability and correct anticipation of the future price level may go together, which is indeed one of the main advantages of price stability, but it is the situation of correct expectations rather than that of price stability *per se* that is reproduced by indexation.[3] By protecting contracts against changes in the value of money, indexation removes most of the uncertainties of inflation and hence the incentive to 'hedge' against inflation by switching into real assets.

---

[1] IEA Occasional Paper 41, 1974.

[2] H. Giersch, 'Index Clauses and the Fight against Inflation', in *Essays on Inflation and Indexation*, Domestic Affairs Studies No. 24, American Enterprise Institute, Washington, DC, 1974.

[3] For example, the introduction of indexation does not rule out *negative* real interest rates (below, p. 39).

Indexation and the economy: some questions

Such a proposal raises a number of questions. Can indexation protect everyone against inflation? Or would it, for example, place a burden on debtors which they could not meet, thus leading to widespread bankruptcies? If indexation can protect everyone, what are the costs? In so far as inflation distorts the allocation of resources, does indexation also offset these distortions, or does it introduce new sources of inefficiency? These questions, which are concerned with the 'welfare economics' of indexation, are discussed in II.

Perhaps more controversial questions relate to the role of indexation in the process of inflation. Does indexation deprive the government of the ability to raise additional tax revenue through inflation? If most contracts are indexed, is there any automatic mechanism to contain an inflationary process once started? What would be the effect of indexation in the context of a 'cost-push' model of the inflationary process? Is it correct to claim that indexation would reduce the costs in terms of unemployment of slowing down inflation? These questions are taken up in III.

In IV we consider the application of indexation to various types of contracts, with particular reference to the tax system and to financial assets, and in V a number of important aspects of the introduction and maintenance of indexation: Would there be transitional problems? What index should be adopted? Does the case for indexation require the comprehensive indexation of all sectors of the economy? Why is indexation not already widespread in the private sector? Is there a case for making indexation of some contracts compulsory?

In VI we discuss issues of economic policy, which necessarily involve political as well as economic considerations. First, we ask whether significant fluctuations in the rate of inflation are likely to be a persistent feature of the economic landscape, for it is in these circumstances that the effects of indexation are of most benefit. We then ask whether, with indexation, inflation would matter. Arguing that it would we then ask whether government would be likely to pursue more inflationary policies than in the absence of indexation. Finally, we ask whether or not indexation would impede the pursuit of other policy objectives in the UK economy at the present time.

Throughout we are concerned with indexation in the context of relatively moderate rates of inflation, in the range suffered by many European nations in recent years and by many Latin American economies over a longer period: that is, with inflation rates at which currency will continue to be used along with other assets, even though currency itself would not be indexed.[1] We do not consider the possibility of hyper-inflation, for it would not seem sensible to set up permanent institutional arrangements to deal with what can only be a short-lived phenomenon. But we might add that anyone who takes the risk of hyper-inflation seriously should also support the introduction of indexation. If indexation preceded hyper-inflation, the ensuing currency reform would not wipe out the value of monetary assets.

Since the Second World War, several countries have adopted indexation of varying degrees of comprehensiveness. (The Bibliography (p. 64) includes references in which this experience is surveyed.)[2] We have refrained from attempting to use this experience as evidence for our arguments. The interpretation of economic history is difficult and complex. We have largely confined ourselves to arguments based on general economic theory, leaving the interpretation of experience overseas to specialists, in accordance with the principle of the division of labour. But we are not aware that evidence on the effects of indexation in other countries conflicts with those we attribute to indexation.

II. INDEXATION AND ECONOMIC WELFARE

In analysing the effects of indexation on economic welfare it is helpful to start by distinguishing between considerations of equity, or income distribution, and of economic efficiency. We first discuss the redistributive effects of inflation, and of indexation. We then examine the efficiency costs of inflation and the extent to which they may be affected by indexation.

Redistribution

Foremost amongst the effects of inflation are the losses suffered by people living on fixed incomes, such as pensioners, small

[1] Like other proponents of indexation, we would not advocate the indexation of currency (VI, section (ii)).

[2] In particular, the sources listed by S. A. B. Page and S. Trollope, 'An International Survey of Indexing and Its Effects', *National Institute Economic Review*, November 1974, p. 60.

savers, holders of government debt and others. The real value of income payments denominated in nominal monetary terms falls as a result of inflation. But the resulting loss to the income recipient is precisely matched by a gain to those making the income payment, who will have to pay less in real terms as a result of inflation.

These effects, then, are redistributions between members of society rather than losses of income to society as a whole. If all such contracts (pensions, mortgages, government debt, etc.) were indexed so that the income payments were denominated in real rather than in monetary terms, their value would be unaffected by inflation. In consequence, those living on fixed incomes would not suffer as a result of inflation, and those making the income payments would no longer gain. This consideration should cast doubt on the proposition that indexed income payment obligations could not be honoured. The effect of indexation of such contracts would be to prevent the losses and the gains that otherwise may arise as a consequence of inflation. Indexation may not create more income for society as a whole, but it eliminates the arbitrary redistributions that may result from inflation.

There can be no doubt that this is one of the most important benefits of indexation. Economists may point out that there are no objective criteria for regarding any one distribution of income in society as inherently preferable to any other, and in consequence no basis for regarding the redistributive effects of inflation as inherently either desirable or undesirable. Yet it seems that such redistributive effects are generally deplored, and regarded as amongst the most harmful effects of inflation. It follows that their elimination by indexation must be regarded as a substantial benefit.

The redistributive effects of inflation also create uncertainty and insecurity. Though in the process of redistribution some lose and some gain, everyone suffers from the uncertainty of not knowing what the future rate of inflation will be, and hence of not knowing how their real income will be affected. If indexation eliminates the redistributive effects of inflation, it will at the same time remove this source of uncertainty. This must be counted a further benefit of indexation.[1]

---

[1] The welfare gain from the reduced worry about the future rate of inflation is in principle distinct from the avoidance of redistributive gains and losses that would otherwise be associated with inflation that has already taken place.

With indexation, everyone can face less uncertainty because the purely redistributive effects of inflation are eliminated. Such effects constitute risks to individuals which do not correspond to risks to society taken as a whole. Hence it is feasible to protect everyone against them. But it may be asked whether or not there are any economic costs in so doing. Many other types of economic uncertainties also have redistributive effects. In principle, it would also be possible to protect people against the purely redistributive effects associated with other economic uncertainties, such as changes in supply and demand. Would this increase economic welfare? Or is there a difference in this respect between inflation and other economic uncertainties?

Inflation is different from other economic uncertainties in this context for two related reasons. First, the redistributive effects of inflation have no function in terms of economic efficiency. That is to say, if there is a monetary disturbance, equilibrium can be restored by a proportional change in all money prices, leaving all *relative* prices, real incomes, etc. unchanged.[1] The distribution of income in the new equilibrium can be the same as in the original position, that is, a redistribution of income is not necessary for the attainment of the new equilibrium. By contrast, other economic uncertainties (changes in tastes, technology, world trading conditions, etc.) will lead to changes in equilibrium relative prices. Such changes in *relative* prices, as readers of *Hobart* and other IEA *Papers* will be aware,[2] perform the essential function of allocating resources among different uses. At the same time they may also lead to redistributions of income. If an attempt were made to avoid these redistributive effects by preventing the change in relative prices, the new equilibrium would not be attained, and prices would not perform their allocative function efficiently.[3]

The related reason for distinguishing inflation from other economic uncertainties is that of incentives for forecasting. In

---

[1] This principle is the 'neutrality of money', a standard proposition of monetary theory which envisages conditions in which the monetary system is such that the supply of money exerts no independent influence on real relative values.

[2] The latest IEA Paper that emphasises the functions of relative prices is F. A. Hayek, *Full Employment at Any Price?*, Occasional Paper 45, 1975.

[3] In principle, relative price changes could take place, and their redistributive effects be offset by lump-sum transfers, but such a policy would scarcely be feasible in practice.

the absence of indexation, individuals will have strong incentives to attempt to predict the future course of inflation, since those who predict correctly can normally benefit at the expense of those who do not. Such forecasting activity, though rewarding to the individual, is socially unproductive, since there is no gain in terms of economic efficiency from the resulting redistributions of income. Indexation would, to a large extent, remove the incentive to individuals to predict the rate of inflation since this would no longer affect the real value of contracts. But if fewer resources were to be directed to forecasting the inflation rate there would be no loss to society since the forecasting is socially unproductive. With other economic uncertainties, by contrast, correct prediction has a social purpose since it can affect the allocation of current resources. Hence, in a market economy, it is efficient that people have incentives to make correct predictions. But if the redistributive effects of any change were neutralised, the incentive would be very much weakened, with adverse effects on the efficiency with which current resources are allocated.

Indexation can therefore, in principle, protect everyone from the redistributive effects of inflation. This is a substantial benefit both insofar as the redistributive effects are regarded as socially unjust, and insofar as it removes a major source of the uncertainty and insecurity now associated with inflation. Furthermore, this result can be achieved at virtually no cost in economic efficiency.[1] But, for the reasons just outlined, indexation can protect people only from the losses and gains due to inflation, not against other economic uncertainties. In particular, indexation should not be seen as a means of guaranteeing real incomes or real purchasing power against every type of economic uncertainty.[2]

Efficiency

While the redistributive effects of inflation are very conspicuous, the losses in economic efficiency are more difficult to identify. Inflation does not, *per se*, appear to reduce the productive capacity of the economy nor, therefore, its real income or

[1] There are, inevitably, some administrative costs of indexation.

[2] Apart from those raised in the text, there are the more obvious considerations that, for example, it is impossible to protect everybody's real income against a contingency which reduces total real income, such as a deterioration in the terms of trade, of which the recent increase in oil prices has been a notable example.

wealth. What are the efficiency costs of inflation? How might they be affected by indexation? The rate of inflation itself is taken as given; whether indexation might affect the rate of inflation is considered in VI.

(A) *Anticipated inflation*

It is helpful to distinguish between efficiency costs that arise even in a fully anticipated inflation, and those due to an incorrect anticipation of the rate of inflation. A fully anticipated inflation is one in which the rate of inflation is always correctly foreseen by everybody. In such a situation the loss of efficiency is limited to two types of effects. One is the incentive to individuals to economise on their holdings of cash balances, though for society as a whole these are not a scarce resource.[1] The other is the costs of frequent changes of prices (which may often be substantial, e.g. as with slot machines, shop labels, rail tickets, etc.). If the costs of changing some prices are high, they will be changed infrequently and in consequence relative prices will be continually moving out of line with their appropriate market values. This leads to a loss of economic efficiency over and above the costs of changing the prices. Even so, for relatively moderate rates of inflation, these costs seem rather small. Furthermore, they could not in any way be avoided by indexation.

There are three conditions for a fully anticipated inflation:

(i) that each individual is certain about the future rate of inflation;

(ii) that all individuals expect the same rate of inflation; and

(iii) that the inflation rate that actually occurs corresponds to that which had been expected.

In an 'unanticipated' inflation one or more of these conditions would not hold, and further efficiency costs may then arise.

(B) *Unanticipated inflation*

First, efficiency costs arise if individuals are uncertain about the future rate of inflation. They will then have an incentive to forecast the inflation rate and thus will consume economic

[1] The idea here is that since cash balances are virtually costless to provide, the cost to individuals of holding cash balances should be correspondingly low. Inflation inflicts a high cost on holding cash balances, since it leads to an erosion of their real value.

resources which might otherwise have been used productively. Further there will be an incentive to hold real rather than monetary assets, insofar as the former provide a hedge against inflation. This course may encourage the production of real assets that are conveniently held directly by households as substitutes for monetary assets (e.g. consumer goods) at the expense of the production of real assets which may be financed through the issue of monetary assets (e.g. productive capital). This process is inefficient if productive capital has a higher real return than stocks of goods.[1] The uncertainty that remains even after these hedging arrangements have been made is itself, of course, also a cost in terms of economic welfare. Indexation is a means of protecting individuals against the uncertainties of inflation (p. 16). It would therefore remove these costs.

Second, if individuals have different expectations about the rate of inflation, future prices expressed in nominal monetary terms will appear to correspond to different real values to individuals with different expectations. It is a necessary condition for the efficient allocation of resources that all individuals face the same set of prices. The rate of interest, for example, is a variable expressed in nominal monetary terms.[2] Given the *nominal* rate of interest in the market, individuals perceive different *real* rates of interest corresponding to their expectations of inflation. Real investment and saving decisions depend, in principle, on the real rate of interest. Individuals with expectations of more rapid inflation, who interpret the nominal interest rate as a relatively low real interest rate, will be prepared to undertake investment projects with a correspondingly low real return. At the same time, capital projects with a higher real rate of return will not be undertaken by individuals expecting a lower rate of inflation.[3] Hence investment funds may be misallocated with a consequent loss of economic efficiency.

[1] In these circumstances, it might be asked why individuals do not switch out of monetary assets into equities, which could finance physical capital formation with no loss of efficiency. Apart from the differential tax treatment, the direct ownership of goods may be less risky than holding equities (particularly in times of political uncertainty, which may often accompany inflation).

[2] This example is due to P. Robson, 'Inflation-Proof Loans', *National Westminster Bank Quarterly Review*, May 1974.

[3] Such individuals will perceive the nominal interest rate as a high real interest rate, and hence will not undertake investment projects unless they offer a correspondingly high return.

Indexation would remove this problem, for it would mean that future prices were denominated in real rather than monetary terms. People with different expectations about the future rate of inflation would expect the monetary payment corresponding to the index adjustment to be different, but everyone would face the same set of prices in real terms. This does, however, require the comprehensive indexation of all contracts (V).

The third feature of unanticipated inflation, that the inflation rate is different from that expected, leads to relatively few costs in economic efficiency. The main problem is that, if some prices are more difficult to adjust than others, relative prices can move away from their appropriate levels, and this leads to a misallocation of resources. If the difficulty of adjustment is due to the high cost of changing the price, indexation will not help, for it cannot reduce it. If, however, the difficulty of adjustment lies in bargaining or negotiating or similar impediments in establishing the price, indexing may help, for those involved may then agree to set an indexed price which will automatically be adjusted to the rate of inflation.

The efficiency costs of unanticipated inflation, like those of anticipated inflation, seem rather small. Furthermore, they do not capture any of the serious problems that inflation creates for the efficient operation of the economy. These problems derive from a different source: the failure of institutional arrangements to be adjusted to inflation. This is particularly, but not exclusively, a defect of the public sector.

Many features of the tax system are denominated in nominal monetary terms (e.g. personal tax allowances). In times of inflation, the effective incidence of the tax structure can be very substantially altered. Likewise prices charged by nationalised industries (and local authorities) are set in money terms, and in real terms are reduced by inflation. The same is true of government pay scales, legal penalties, etc.

The question, of course, is why such tax allowances, prices, etc. cannot be adjusted with inflation. The difficulty seems to lie in the persistence of some form of 'money illusion' in the political process. For example, to maintain the real level of council house rents will require an increase in nominal monetary terms. This would provoke a political debate over whether rents should be 'increased' (when the issue in real terms is whether or not they are to be reduced) with all the political emotion that such a debate ferments. Similarly, to maintain the existing degree of progressiveness of the income tax system requires an increase, in nominal monetary terms, of the starting points for the higher rates of tax, and this will appear as a concession (or 'hand-out') to the wealthy.

If the original structure of taxes, and government pricing, is taken as reflecting social objectives, in some sense, it follows that the inability to maintain it in times of inflation can lead to substantial losses in social welfare. For example, the reduction in the real level of controlled rents induced by inflation must have exacerbated the present housing shortage. Similarly, charging corporation tax on stock appreciation in nominal terms can lead to the bankruptcy of otherwise perfectly viable trading enterprises.

Indexation might alleviate these problems if the 'money illusion' which prevents the adjustments of nominal values represents genuine confusion on the part of the public. For indexation makes explicit what part of any change in nominal values is due to a change in real values, and what part is due to inflation. Indexation would also help if, by making adjustments automatic, it removed them from the political debate. But if the 'money illusion' takes the form of general public refusal to see increases in nominal public sector prices, even when they do no more than reflect the rate of inflation, then indexation would not solve this problem, for the rise in prices in nominal terms would continue to be unacceptable. In such circumstances, politicians will be reluctant to introduce indexation, since it would deprive them of the freedom to choose when to introduce price increases.

These problems of adjustment to inflation apply also to private institutions such as building societies and pension funds. The reluctance to adjust them seems again mainly due to 'money illusion' in the sense of an unwillingness to abandon old habits of thought and established commercial practice. There are also some more detailed problems (IV).

Thus it cannot be claimed that indexation would remove all the efficiency losses due to inflation. But it can be claimed that some of them would be removed. Indexation is not of itself totally without cost, since it inevitably entails administrative costs. Nonetheless, in an inflationary economy, indexation can make a significant contribution to reducing the efficiency costs attributable to inflation.

Together with the more clear-cut equity gains of indexation, this conclusion seems to indicate clearly that the welfare costs of inflation can be significantly and substantially reduced by indexation. In the popular expression, indexation would make it 'easier to live with inflation'.

III. INDEXATION AND THE PROCESS OF INFLATION

We now consider four main issues connected with the effects of indexation:

(i) Would indexation deprive the government of the ability to acquire resources through inflation?

(ii) Would indexation undermine the automatic tendency of rising prices to check inflation?

(iii) Would indexation aggravate inflation in the face of 'cost-push' pressures?

(iv) Would indexation reduce the costs, in unemployment, of slowing down inflation?

(i) *Inflation and Tax Revenue*

We have considered whether the protection offered by indexation against the redistributions which may result from inflation entails resource costs for society. Although the answer to this question is 'No', it might still be held that indexation involves a 'cost' if it deprives government of an instrument, namely inflation, for the acquisition of additional resources. We will now briefly analyse how inflation may transfer additional resources from the private to the public sector, and how this process would be affected by indexation.[1]

It is generally agreed that in all sustained inflations the public's nominal currency holdings rise faster than output. By expanding the nominal amount of currency outstanding, the government always acquires additional resources,[2] and the faster the rate of currency creation relative to the real growth

---

[1] This question is discussed in Friedman, *op. cit.*, pp. 14-15.

[2] If one asks who exactly provides these resources to the government, the answer is *all* holders of currency, who are worse off in so far as the real value per nominal unit of their currency holdings is diminished.

rate of the economy, the larger the share of national income transferred to the government by this inflation tax. Since the indexation of currency is not envisaged, this mechanism of transferring resources from the private to the public sector would not be affected by indexation.

The question whether inflation transfers resources from the private sector to the government, apart from the inflation tax on currency holdings, is the same as whether there is 'fiscal drag'.[1] We propose to consider some examples to indicate what is at issue.

On the side of government revenue, let us take the example of income tax. With a progressive income tax, and with tax brackets fixed in nominal terms, the share of government revenue in real national income will rise with the rate of inflation. For some tax-payers this is because the real value of allowances falls, thus raising the average rate of tax on a given real income. For others it is because they are also pushed into higher tax brackets, thus becoming subject to higher average and marginal rates of tax on any given real income.

In what sense is this increase in average and marginal real tax rates to be attributed to inflation? Presumably only if it is held that, in the absence of inflation, the government would have regarded itself as unable, or would have been unwilling, to impose the same *real* tax rates as prevail when inflation takes place and the tax brackets are fixed in nominal terms. Thus the question whether this transfer of resources is to be attributed to inflation is a matter of political rather than economic interpretation, which is not to suggest that economists can afford to neglect it.

If the political decision-making process is subject to some kind of 'money illusion', real tax revenue will depend on the rate of inflation. Indexation would break this link. As a result, less real resources might be made available to the government through taxation.[2] Is this to be counted as an argument against

---

[1] 'Fiscal drag' is the term used to describe the process whereby a government's nominal tax receipts rise faster than prices in times of inflation, due to the progressiveness of the tax system in nominal terms, thus leading to an increase in real tax revenues.

[2] The discussion relates to the example of a progressive income-tax structure. It does not imply that the structure of the UK tax system gives rise to 'fiscal drag'. Unit taxes, fixed in nominal monetary terms, such as excise duties or alcohol and tobacco, provide a lower real yield when prices rise. Whether total real tax revenues rise as a result of inflation is therefore an empirical question.

indexation, for example on the ground that it might prevent the government from pursuing 'socially desirable' expenditure policies?

Those who advocate government expenditures which they believe can be financed only by inflation, cannot also oppose inflation on the ground that it leads to higher taxes. We shall have occasion to repeat this proposition, which is one of logical consistency. It may also be argued that, in a democratic society, there is something unsatisfactory about the notion that certain government expenditures are 'socially desirable' even though they can be financed only as a result of some kind of 'money illusion'. Indeed on these grounds indexation should be regarded as desirable as it would prevent an expansion of real government expenditure simply as a result of inflation.

Apart from the possible effect of inflation on the real value of government tax revenue, inflation will also affect the real value of payment on outstanding government debt. Two effects should be noted here. First, a rate of inflation higher than anticipated by borrowers when the debt was issued will clearly reduce the real amount of interest and redemption payments. Second, even if the now higher rate of inflation comes to be anticipated, the government may be able to place new issues at a lower expected real interest rate, because the earlier unanticipated inflation will have reduced the real value of the National Debt. Once again, if indexation were adopted, inflation would no longer bring about these two effects. Those who wish to regard this as a 'cost' of indexation cannot also disapprove of the effects of inflation on the holders of government debt.

(ii) *The Containment of Inflation*

We have considered in what sense it might be said that inflation may help government to acquire more resources. A related question is whether indexation, by preventing the redistribution which may occur automatically in its absence, may not make it more difficult to contain inflation once it has developed.

It is helpful to distinguish three questions:

(*a*) Do the automatic redistributions which inflation may bring about *within* the private sector help to contain inflation by reducing demand?

(*b*) Do the redistributions between the private and public sector, discussed in (i), help to reduce demand? and

[25]

(c)   Even if the answers to (a) and (b) were 'Yes', are these the only means of reducing demand to contain inflation?

In answer to (a), various affirmative suggestions have been made, particularly in the context of the Keynesian income-expenditure theory. If wages lagged behind prices, for example, there would be a shift to profits, and if profit receivers saved more from an additional unit of income than did wage earners, the shift to profits would diminish total consumption demand at any level of income, thus reducing the inflationary gap. Similarly, as discussed in II, net monetary creditors would lose to the benefit of net monetary debtors,[1] and if the expenditure reactions of these two groups to changes in their wealth were different, there might be a reduction in total demand. Since indexation would prevent these redistributions, it might be argued that rising prices would no longer help to reduce demand.

There is an important difference between the two examples. The reduction in (real) wages is due to the inflation having been unanticipated, and (assuming no change in the productivity of labour) competition will soon restore real wages to their magnitude before prices rose. Thus, the fall in real wages (even granting that workers save less than profit receivers) can reduce demand only temporarily,[2] and is thus not a mechanism which could check inflation. Indexation would indeed prevent the temporary reduction in real wages, but would not impair a non-existent inflation-dampening mechanism.

The transfer of wealth from net monetary creditors to net monetary debtors is indeed permanent, unless reversed by a subsequent unanticipated deflation, but does not necessarily reduce demand. We must therefore conclude that, despite the attention given to these factors in the early post-war literature, it is an open question whether such redistributions would themselves help to contain inflation. But even if they did, we must repeat that it is illogical simultaneously to deplore the redistributive effects of inflation but applaud their demand-reducing effects, since the latter depend on the former.

[1] Net monetary creditors are those whose monetary assets exceed their monetary liabilities, and net monetary debtors those whose monetary liabilities exceed their monetary assets. Monetary assets are assets whose value is fixed in nominal monetary terms, or which entitle their holders to an income fixed in nominal monetary terms, and likewise for monetary liabilities.

[2] This mechanism also assumes that the individuals affected do not realise that these changes are temporary.

(*b*). This question, at first sight, appears to be the same as that discussed in (i). While the two are clearly related, there is an important difference between them. In so far as inflation automatically provides government with additional resources which it proceeds to spend on current output, this transfer will not reduce demand. Total demand would be reduced only if government increased its demand for current output by less than the reduction of demand in the private sector resulting from the inflation-induced transfers to the government. It is therefore possible that these automatic transfers may have an inflation-dampening effect.

(*c*). It follows from our earlier discussion of 'fiscal drag' that these automatic redistributions are not the only means of reducing real demand. If they reduce demand, so will tax increases. It is therefore not clear why advocates of fiscal Keynesian-style stabilisation policies should wish to rely on these automatic effects, unless because of the political constraints on budgetary policy mentioned in (i), particularly when these automatic effects have consequences deemed undesirable.

Finally, it must be emphasised that one of the major—perhaps *the*—automatic dampening effects would be unaffected by indexation, namely the effect of rising prices on the real value of currency holdings.

(iii) *'Cost-push' Inflation*

It is sometimes claimed that indexation would lead to accelerating inflation. Such claims may be based on a 'cost-push' model of the inflationary process. We now examine this model and ask what would happen if indexation were introduced.

Friedman summarises the cost-push model thus:

'. . . . inflation serves the critical social purpose of resolving incompatible demands by different groups. To put it crudely, the participants in the economy have "non-negotiable demands" for more than the whole output.'[1]

On the basis of this approach, the National Institute of Economic and Social Research has argued that, if indexation were introduced, there might still be

[1] M. Friedman, *op. cit.*, p. 31. Friedman does not endorse the cost-push argument.

'. . . a sum of claims on output which exceeded that likely to be available at unchanged prices. The struggle for "shares of the cake" might even be intensified in the absence of the soothing agency of "money illusion". This is another way of saying that indexation might intensify inflation rather than moderate it.'[1]

In effect, it is being asserted that workers, capitalists, and others with claims on output jointly demand more than one unit of output for each unit produced. But what does this mean for the individual firm? Does the argument imply that firms are typically prepared to concede claims for money incomes which in total amount to more than the receipts from the sale of their product at unchanged prices?

We may interpret the 'struggle for shares' in the individual firm as follows: each group of participants in the production process (workers, capitalists, etc.) insists both that the firm maintain the existing level of production, employment, etc. and that it pays incomes to those participants which amount to more than the firm's sales receipts at unchanged prices. How can a firm agree to meet such claims? Where does it expect to get the money from to honour these agreements?

There are only three possibilities: additional output, higher prices, or non-commercial sources of funds. If firms believe that, for example, whatever contracts they enter into, the government will always bail them out, and if such a belief is justified, there seems no limit to the claims that would be made and met, and it is hard to see how the outcome of such a process could be anything other than runaway inflation.

Second, firms may agree to the income claims because they expect a faster rate of growth of output than those making the claims. While presumably this is always possible, it is hard to believe that such differential expectations will persist systematically over time. Firms that are persistently over-optimistic about their productivity growth, and agree to make income payments on this basis, will soon become bankrupt.

These possibilities, then, seem implausible as explanations of any general tendency for firms to agree to income claims in excess of their sales receipts at unchanged prices. Presumably, the general explanation is that firms expect to be able to increase their sales receipts by raising their prices. But if firms

[1] *National Institute Economic Review*, November 1974, p. 39.

are maximising their profits, an increase in prices will not lead to an increase in sales receipts, since a price increase reduces demand for the product. It is only if a firm expects a *general* increase of prices in the economy, i.e. inflation, that it can increase its prices without losing its customers, and hence increase its sales receipts. That is to say, firms can agree to pay income claims in excess of sales receipts at current prices *only if they expect inflation*. The existence of such incompatible claims must therefore be regarded as a symptom rather than a cause of inflation.

Further, the mechanism depends on workers, and others with claims on output, being fooled by inflation into believing that their real demands are being met by an increase in money wages when in truth they are not. This is the reference to 'money illusion' in the NIESR quotation (p. 28). The assumption that, for moderate rates of inflation, workers will not learn from experience and come to anticipate continuing inflation is of course absurd, and clearly refuted by recent experience in Britain. If workers come to anticipate inflation in their wage demands, only ever-accelerating inflation can maintain the illusion, and this can hardly be regarded as a tolerable solution. If this model is indeed a description of the inflationary process, we can only accept Friedman's conclusion that there can be '. . . no ultimate outcome other than either runaway inflation or an authoritarian society.'[1, 2]

But if this description of the process is correct, what would happen if indexation were introduced? The explanation of the process we have outlined could not work. Firms could no longer concede wage demands in the expectation that they would be eroded by inflation since, with indexation, inflation would not erode the real value of wage settlements. With indexation, firms would not be in a position to accede to such wage demands.

It follows that, if demands are genuinely 'incompatible' and 'non-negotiable', it will be impossible to introduce indexation. No indexed contracts will ever be agreed on. If, on the other

---

[1] M. Friedman, *op. cit.*, p. 32.

[2] The above claim should not be taken to imply that we believe runaway inflation could occur irrespective of what happens to the money supply. Rather, we merely wish to point to a logical consequence of the cost-push theory. If restricting the money supply can prevent runaway inflation, this would lead one to question the postulate of the model according to which the irreconcilable demands are non-negotiable.

hand, demands are not incompatible, indexation could be introduced, but then it is not possible to argue that indexation might worsen inflation on the grounds of incompatible demands. In short, the fears expressed in the NIESR quotation appear to be groundless.

It is sometimes suggested that incomes policies are required to ensure that the sum of claims for increases in real income does not exceed the likely rise in real output. It is not clear how incomes policies can achieve this result if the sum of demands is 'excessive' and the demands themselves 'non-negotiable'. We have shown that, if indexed contracts are voluntarily agreed, the sum of demands will be compatible with what is available. Hence there can be no justification, on these grounds, for suggesting that indexation would need to be accompanied by any form of incomes policy.

Is indexation a form of incomes policy?

At this stage it might be appropriate to comment on what appears to be a widespread confusion, namely that indexation is in itself a form of incomes policy.[1] There is, of course, no similarity whatsoever between the two. Indexation means that wage bargains are struck in terms of money of constant purchasing power (as they would be in times of price stability); it does not imply any interference in the determination of the size of wage settlements.[2] Thus indexation is not in any way inconsistent with the working of market forces, or of collective bargaining. There is no reason therefore to expect that indexation would lead to either the market distortions or the political hostility which inevitably accompany incomes policies. In V we briefly consider whether trade unions have good reason to be opposed to indexation.

The 'dilemma'

Another source of misgivings about the effects of indexation is the so-called 'dilemma model': trade unions attempt to achieve

[1] As it has been in Brazil. For this reason we would not cite the Brazilian experience in support of our arguments for indexation of wages.

[2] Statutory indexation of wages means that wages would have to be indexed, but does not in any way affect the size of wage settlements that could be reached. Thus, unlike statutory incomes policy, it does not fix relative prices by statute, or, therefore, interfere with allocative efficiency. Cf. C. G. Fane, 'Index-linking and Inflation', *National Institute Economic Review*, November 1974, p. 44.

money wage increases incompatible with the maintenance of full employment, given the prevailing price level. The government is then faced with the dilemma of either validating the increases by expansionary monetary policy or of allowing unemployment to rise. This picture of the economy has some features in common with that of the 'cost-push' model discussed above, namely the (alleged) unwillingness of workers to accept the real wages which are compatible with full employment, and the allegedly soothing effect of inflation in persuading workers that they are receiving higher real wages than they are. If indexation were to be introduced in such a situation it would lead to the same unemployment which would result if the government refused to validate the increases in money wages. Hence the suggestion that, in order to avoid the unemployment, indexation would need to be accompanied by an incomes policy designed to persuade workers to accept the real wages which are compatible with full employment.

Our comments on the 'dilemma model' are, at bottom, the same as those on the 'cost-push' model. Continuing inflation will secure full employment only so long as workers do not realise it is taking place. This is an absurd supposition. If workers still insist on trying to obtain real wages in excess of those compatible with full employment, full employment could be maintained only at the cost of ever-accelerating inflation, which is not a viable full employment policy.

According to the 'cost-push' model people will accept their share of income only if they are deceived about it; according to the 'dilemma model', workers will accept the real wages compatible with full employment only if they are deceived about them. It is not clear how incomes policy will teach people to accept the situation as it is. The case for indexation does indeed rest on the assumption that people need not be deceived about the situation in which they find themselves.

(iv) The Expectations Theory of Inflation

If a 'struggle for shares' is the explanation of inflation, the introduction of indexation would be impossible and the inevitable outcome would be runaway inflation. If the 'dilemma' model were correct, full employment could be maintained only at the cost of ever-accelerating inflation. Fortunately, as we have suggested, these theories are so implausible as not to warrant serious consideration. We prefer the explanation of inflation couched in terms of changes in aggregate monetary demand and in expectations, and propose to discuss the effects of indexation in its light.

Our main contention will be that indexation would ease the difficulties of slowing down the rate of inflation.

In reaching agreements, people will take into account their expectations of the course of the price level (II). In particular, wage contracts will incorporate expectations of the future rate of inflation. We may begin by considering a situation in which a high rate of inflation has persisted for some time and is widely expected to continue. Let us suppose that people's expectations of the rate of inflation have been correct. If the rate of inflation were allowed to continue, the introduction of indexation would in no way change the situation. While previously money wage settlements would have incorporated expected inflation, with indexation money wages would rise with the rate of inflation, which we have supposed to be the same.

Suppose the rate of inflation had been proceeding steadily at 25 per cent. If the government wished to reduce it to, say, 10 per cent and had some means whereby it could simultaneously induce the population to *expect* a 10 per cent rate of inflation, money wages and prices would rise 15 per cent less than before, and output and employment would be unaffected. The difficulty is that there seems to be no means whereby the government can affect people's expectations in this way. As far as is known, people's expectations of inflation seem to derive largely from their recent experience of inflation, rather than from government promises.[1]

If this is true, consider the difficulty faced by a government intent on reducing the rate of inflation by orthodox deflationary policies. Whilst monetary demand will fall, increases in money wages, to begin with at any rate, will be maintained at their previous rate.[2] In these circumstances the reduction in price increases will be smaller than when people's expectations are adjusted completely to changes in government policy, *and* there will be effects on output and employment.

In the context of a policy designed to reduce the rate of inflation, indexation thus has two inter-related aims:

[1] J. A. Carlson and Michael Parkin, 'Inflation Expectations', *Economica*, May 1975.

[2] This mechanism is not to be confused with the cost-push mechanism (pp. 29-31). In the present case both workers and employers continue, for the time being at any rate, to expect an *unchanged* rate of inflation.

(*a*) to prevent prevailing expectations of inflation from influencing the outcome of wage settlements and thus contributing to the continuation of inflation by the 'strong tendency to build the inflation rate of the past into the new collective agreements',[1] and

(*b*) to obviate the need for changing people's expectations of inflation since, according to the expectations theory, this in general requires an increase in unemployment.

We shall now discuss these two objectives of indexation in more detail.

(*a*) Wage settlements are made for varying periods. In the absence of indexation, but in the presence of expectations of future inflation, workers can protect themselves against future inflation only by seeking settlements which incorporate those expectations.

Indexation of wages and salaries makes it possible to arrive at wage settlements which do not reflect expectations of future inflation—however widespread these may be—but which at the same time protect workers from the effects of inflation subsequent to any wage settlement. In other words, by adjusting wages to *realised* rather than to *anticipated* inflation, indexation would make expectations of inflation irrelevant to wage settlements.[2]

(*b*) In the absence of indexation, according to the expectations theory, it is necessary to reduce the rate of inflation workers expect if any given level of employment is to be maintained with a lower rate of inflation. This requires that the *actual* rate of inflation be reduced below the expected rate, which, in turn, requires a temporary fall in employment.

This argument, although it contains a number of unresolved difficulties,[3] is gaining acceptance amongst economists. An obvious implication is that, with indexation, workers' expectations of inflation will not affect the outcome of wage settlements. It is therefore unnecessary to change these expectations in order to reduce the rate of inflation, and hence unnecessary to create 'temporary' unemployment for this purpose.

[1] H. Giersch, *op. cit.*, p. 6.

[2] This consideration is sometimes overlooked, for example when indexation of wages and salaries is urged as part of a policy package in which 'The critical element is a clear advance announcement of the inflation rate to be expected . . .'. (G. L. Bach, *The New Inflation*, Prentice-Hall Inc., New Jersey, 1973, p. 75.)

[3] J. Tobin, 'Inflation and Unemployment', *American Economic Review*, March 1972.

This argument has a further implication, which should be emphasised. According to the expectations theory, the government can temporarily reduce the level of unemployment by raising the actual inflation rate above the expected rate. The level of unemployment would be reduced for the same reasons that it would be raised if the government reduced the actual below the expected inflation rate in the absence of indexation. With indexation the level of employment becomes independent of both the actual and expected inflation rates, and such manoeuvres by the government would cease to work. Thus indexation would deprive the government of one of the main incentives to pursue inflationary policies.

The whole of this argument, however, has been based on the assumption that a change in aggregate monetary demand leads in the first instance to a change in prices, and that it is the lag between the adjustment of prices and the adjustment of wages that is responsible for the effects on output and employment. But it can be argued, and there is empirical support for such an argument, that in practice both wages and prices are inflexible in the short run, and the changes in aggregate monetary demand in the first instance influence output and employment without any change in either wages or prices. It has sometimes been suggested that, in these circumstances, indexation would not reduce the unemployment associated with a slowing down of the rate of inflation.

If the rate of growth of the money supply were reduced, the short-run effect would be a reduction in output and employment, with no effect on wages or prices. Since prices are unaffected, indexation would have no effect at this stage.[1] In the long run, however, wages and prices would respond to the reduction in demand, and once this starts to happen the indexation arrangements would again lead to a more rapid deceleration of the increase in wages, and hence in prices. Again, the slower rate of price increases would be more quickly transmitted to a slower rate of growth in money wages than in the absence of indexation, and therefore the process of reducing inflation would require less unemployment.

We would conclude therefore that, in an economy character-

---

[1] For this reason it is sometimes suggested that wages be indexed to the money supply. In the short run, the velocity of circulation of money, the relationship between the money stock and the level of money income, is too unstable to make this idea feasible.

ised by generalised price inflexibility, indexation would not deprive government of the opportunity to reduce unemployment in the short run. Hence, we must be sceptical of any claim that indexation must be expected to lead the government to adopt a more deflationary monetary policy.[1] At the same time, even in circumstances of generalised price inflexibility it remains true that indexation would reduce the costs in unemployment of slowing down the rate of inflation.

IV. INDEXATION AND SPECIFIC CONTRACTS

How would indexation operate in practice? We do not propose to discuss the administrative problems in detail, but rather to indicate how indexation in specific cases would have to operate if it were to achieve the objectives we have discussed. We start with the government.

The tax system

The purpose of indexing the tax system is to ensure that the effective incidence on taxpayers, in real terms, is unaffected by inflation. This serves objectives of constitutionality, i.e. that taxes should be imposed by overt legislative action rather than surreptitiously through inflation, and of removing the inequities and inefficiencies that may otherwise arise.

The main requirement is therefore that, throughout the tax system, whenever a figure or value is expressed in nominal monetary terms it should be indexed to maintain its real value.[2] This procedure would entail:

(i) in the personal income tax, indexing the personal allowances, starting points for the higher tax brackets, the threshhold for the investment income surcharge, etc.;

(ii) in the capital gains, capital transfer, and (proposed) wealth taxes, indexing the exemption limits and tax brackets;

[1] This claim has been attributed, incorrectly, to Friedman, e.g. by Yang, *op. cit.*, p. 4. But Friedman's claim that indexation 'will make it politically feasible to end inflation' (*op. cit.*, p. 32) implies a belief that a deflationary policy would be more likely with indexation than without it.

[2] A comprehensive list of the figures involved is in H. Hudson, 'The Indexation of the Tax System', in Thelma Liesner and M. King (eds.), *Indexing for Inflation*, Institute for Fiscal Studies, 1975.

[35]

(iii) in indirect taxation, indexing the excise duties on petrol, tobacco and alcohol, motor vehicle licence duties, etc.;

(iv) in the rating system, indexing rateable values.

The main practical problem is that if nominal values in a financial year are to be adjusted to an index of prices ruling in that year, they cannot be known at the beginning of that year. But unless the inflation rate were highly volatile, it might be sufficient to index on the basis of the previous year's inflation rate. All tax allowances, etc. for the financial year 1976-7 would be increased relative to those for 1975-6 by the amount by which the price index had risen between, say, February 1975 and February 1976 (or whatever were the latest figures at the beginning of the 1976-7 financial year).

A second requirement of indexing the tax system is to avoid taxing nominal capital gains as if they were real. This occurs with capital gains tax, corporation tax and, less obviously, with the taxation of income derived from monetary assets. With capital gains tax the remedy, in principle, is straightforward. The tax should be levied only on 'real' gains, so the acquisition value of the asset should be adjusted upwards in nominal terms in proportion to the rise in the price index. The tax would then be charged on the real gain, i.e. the difference between the sale price and the inflation-adjusted purchase price. The same principle would apply to corporation tax insofar as it is levied on nominal gains, e.g. stock appreciation.[1] With income taxation the problem is more complex. Insofar as the interest paid on monetary assets serves simply to compensate their holders for the reduction in their real value as a result of inflation, it should not be liable to tax. It is difficult to see how, exactly, such an arrangement could be made in the income-tax system. Indexing the assets themselves would solve the problem (p. 38). A similar problem arises with interest payments on nominal monetary liabilities. Insofar as,

[1] The heated debate on the appropriate tax treatment of stock appreciation in the UK was concerned not so much with the issue in principle, which is our concern, but rather with the question whether the corporate sector should be exempted from taxation on nominal stock appreciation when it was not liable to taxation on the real gains accruing from the reduction in the real value of its outstanding monetary debt. (A. J. Merrett and A. Sykes, 'The real crisis now facing Britain's Industry', *Financial Times*, 30 September 1974, and W. A. H. Godley and A. Wood, 'Uses and Abuses of Stock Appreciation', *The Times*, 12 November 1974.)

in times of inflation, such payments simply compensate for the falling real value of the monetary debt, they represent a repayment of capital and should not, therefore, be tax deductible. This problem would also be overcome by indexing the debt.[1]

Finally, we consider 'cumulative' taxes, such as the new capital transfer tax. An individual's liability to capital transfer tax on a gift depends on the accumulated total of his gifts to that date. If such a cumulation is made in nominal monetary terms, it will underestimate the real value of gifts made in the past, and will operate inequitably between taxpayers. The individual's previous gifts, like the exemption limits of the tax, should be indexed, so that the real tax yield on future gifts is independent of the rate of inflation.

Government debt

The purpose of indexing government debt is to ensure that the real return to the holders is independent of the rate of inflation. Inflation has two types of effects on the return stream on monetary assets. Not only, as is well known, does it affect the real value of the return stream, but also, insofar as the inflation is expected, it alters the expected distribution over time of the real income payments on the assets. In times of price stability, fixed interest stocks offer a constant real income stream; in times of inflation the real income diminishes over time. To the extent that expected inflation is reflected in the nominal interest rate, interest payments on the asset are higher in the earlier years, and lower in the later years of its life, than they would have been had prices been stable. This 'front-loading' effect itself can have serious consequences for the liquidity position of monetary debtors.[2] It is desirable, therefore, that the form of indexation should be one which would remove this 'front-loading' effect as well as protecting the real value of the return stream.

[1] Under current legislation this difficulty does not in any case exist in the personal sector, where interest payments other than on mortgages are not tax deductible. There is, however, a tax advantage to the corporate sector (footnote, p. 36).

[2] For example, of those who have taken out mortgages. This would not be a problem if the relevant capital markets were perfect, for then the borrower could always borrow more in the earlier period of the loan and repay more in the later period. In practice, most capital markets cannot be regarded as perfect in this respect.

To achieve these objectives, indexation would take the following form. If the government were to issue, say, a 20-year stock with a real interest rate of 2 per cent, it would promise to pay, for each £100 nominal value of stock, £2 per year multiplied by the ratio of the price index of that year to the price index of the year of issue, and on maturity £100 multiplied by the ratio of the price index of that year to the price index of the year of issue. Thus the stock would pay a constant real income stream over time, and at redemption the real value of the principle would be repaid.[1]

The main difficulty associated with the introduction of indexed bonds is their effect on the prices of existing (unindexed) stock. While concern over this possibility is mainly relevant to the transition from an unindexed to a largely indexed economy (V), it does raise two issues of more general significance. One is the question of how the existence of indexed stock affects the prices and yields of other assets, and the other is the question whether indexed stock rules out the possibility of negative real interest rates.

On the first point, it might be expected that indexed bonds would sell at a premium over unindexed bonds with the same expected return, since the real income stream on indexed bonds unaffected by inflation is subject to less uncertainty.[2] But this does not imply that the prices of unindexed bonds will be lower than they would have been in the absence of the indexed bond. The price of unindexed bonds is determined by the real rate of interest prevailing in the economy, the expected rate of inflation, and the extent of risk aversion to inflation. It is only if the introduction of the indexed bond affects any of these factors that it will affect the price of existing unindexed bonds.

The most important effect would be that of indexation on the expected rate of inflation. The direction of this effect is not

---

[1] This means that the protection of the capital value of the asset against inflation takes the form of nominal capital gains rather than of income payments, which clarifies the position for tax purposes (previous section).

[2] J. H. Yang has pointed out an interesting qualification to this argument. The 'front-loading' effect on the unindexed bonds effectively shortens their lives and this means less capital uncertainty in the sense that the capital values of such bonds would be affected to a smaller extent by changes in the real interest rate. This qualification is likely to be of minor significance in practice: J. H. Yang, 'The Case For and Against Indexation: An Attempt at Perspective', *Federal Reserve Bank of St. Louis Review*, October 1974, pp. 8-9.

clear. In VI we examine the question whether indexation would be likely to lead to a faster or a slower rate of inflation and conclude that either outcome would be possible. The effect on the inflation risk discount on unindexed bonds is more subtle. If the government issues indexed rather than unindexed debt, the supply of assets whose value is secured in real terms would rise, and hence the premium they would attract would tend to fall. This would tend to reduce the discount due to aversion to the risk of inflation on unindexed bonds, and hence tend to increase their prices. (For the same reason the price of real assets which had been in particular demand as a 'hedge' against inflation might tend to fall because indexed bonds increase the supply of inflation-proof assets.)

Secondly, would indexation rule out the possibility of negative real interest rates? If indexed bonds were issued when nominal interest rates were below the generally expected rate of inflation, they would attract a premium over their par value, such that they would also be offering a negative real return. (It is possible to imagine indexed bonds being issued with a negative coupon, but for obvious administrative reasons they would be ruled out.) Indexed bonds are thus perfectly consistent with negative real interest rates.

Though negative real interest rates may co-exist with indexed bonds, they may not be consistent with more widespread indexation. This would depend on the factor responsible for the negative real interest rates. In general, one possible explanation might be the heavy effective taxation of capital in times of inflation. If the tax system were indexed this tax effect would not occur, and this would rule out one possible cause of negative real interest rates. Insofar as this consequence of indexing the tax system led to higher real interest rates, it would not, however, lead to lower bond prices, for the higher interest rate would be offset by a lower tax liability (since the maintenance of the real capital value would no longer attract a tax liability).

We may conclude that, unless indexation were to be accompanied by an expectation of a faster rate of inflation, it would not significantly affect the prices of unindexed securities.[1]

---

[1] S. Fischer, 'The Demand for Index Bonds', *Journal of Political Economy*, June 1975, contains a rigorous analysis of this problem. We have not had time to study this article carefully, but a cursory reading suggests that his conclusions are not inconsistent with those stated here.

This conclusion seems to differ from that generally reached.[1] The general conclusion seems to be asserted rather than argued, and hence it is difficult to pinpoint the source of the difference.

National savings

Apart from marketable fixed-interest debt, the government also borrows by issuing non-negotiable debt of fixed nominal capital value, usually intended primarily for 'small savers'.

If indexation were introduced, National Savings instruments would also be indexed. There is no difficulty in doing this, provided the real rate of interest elsewhere in the economy is positive. If, however, indexed National Savings are issued at a time when real interest rates are negative[2] there would be a problem, since the government may find it inexpedient to offer an explicitly negative real return on National Savings. The British government has, indeed, been offering negative real returns for many years, but indexation would make this situation explicit. It is not clear that, as has sometimes been suggested,[3] no-one would be prepared to take up such issues, for people are often aware that their savings provide a negative real return. Rather the difficulty is that the government may wish to avoid giving the impression that it is party to the expropriation of small savers. In such circumstances, the government is likely to issue the indexed National Savings at a zero or even slightly positive real interest rate, but severely ration the issue. Such a procedure may serve the limited distributional objective of helping small savers. But rationing of such issues is scarcely consistent with the general purpose of indexation, which is to assist rather than restrict the operation of markets.

We turn now to the private sector.

Commercial debt

Commercial debentures could be indexed in the same way as government fixed-interest securities. This reform would enable businesses to borrow long-term again, which becomes impossible during inflation due to the risks involved and the 'front-loading' effect.

[1] E.g., N. F. Althaus, 'Indexation and the Capital Market', in Liesner and King, *op. cit.*, p. 95; also below, footnote 3, p. 44.

[2] As with indexed National Savings in the UK at the time of writing.

[3] P. Robson, *op. cit.*, p. 54.

It is sometimes suggested that businessmen would fear to issue indexed debt as this would entail an open-ended commitment in nominal monetary terms. As stated, this fear is not sensible, since businessmen are more concerned with real than with monetary variables, and the indexed debt entails a fixed commitment in real terms. But given a large government sector operating in nominal monetary terms, the fear may not be so unreasonable (V).

Banks

Bank deposit and overdraft rates could be indexed. This again might present difficulties in times of negative real interest rates when, for example, a bank might offer a return on deposit accounts equal to the rate of inflation less 5 per cent or less 10 per cent. If there were to be a reform of banking practice, such that banks were to offer explicit interest payments on current account, and make explicit charges for their services,[1] such interest payments could also be indexed.

Building societies

Mortgage finance is particularly vulnerable to the difficulty presented by 'front-loading'. Many people taking out mortgages are of relatively modest means, and find it difficult to borrow except through specific financial intermediaries such as building societies. For example, consider an individual taking out a 25-year mortgage at, say, a 1 per cent *real* interest rate. With stable prices, repayments in the first year would amount to approximately $4\frac{1}{2}$ per cent of the amount borrowed. If there is then 20 per cent inflation, but the real interest rate remains at 1 per cent, the nominal interest rate will rise to 21 per cent and hence repayments in the first year would amount to approximately 21 per cent of the amount borrowed. This may constitute an immense liquidity problem for potential house purchasers.

Under indexation, the borrower would be charged a 1 per cent interest rate, but the mortgage debt would be indexed. Thus the repayment in the first year would again be $4\frac{1}{2}$ per cent of the amount borrowed, but the repayment would

[1] Brian Griffiths, *Competition in Banking*, Hobart Paper 51, IEA, 1970, pp. 34-5.

then increase in nominal monetary terms by 20 per cent per year (and thus remain constant in real terms).[1] There can be no doubt that this liquidity problem is in large part responsible for the current state of the housing market in the UK, which remains depressed despite substantially negative real interest rates on mortages.

Indexation would temporarily reduce building societies' receipts from repayments on mortgages outstanding. Provided they offered 'competitive' interest rates to their depositors, there should not be financial difficulties for them, because they could borrow adequately on the strength of their expected receipts. Building societies have also objected to indexed mortgages on the ground that a mortgage declining in real terms may be what borrowers really want. Whatever the merits of such an argument, we may simply note that building societies were not persuaded by them to introduce a declining real mortgage arrangement in times of price stability.

Pension funds

The objective is to index pensions, so that pensioners are protected against inflation. For the pension funds, indexed pensions represent indexed liabilities, which they have been unwilling to take on in the absence of any indexed assets to hold against such liabilities. This difficulty would clearly be overcome by the more general availability of indexed financial assets.

Wages and salaries

Finally, we consider an area in which indexation is required to serve a rather different purpose.

The objective is to make expectations of inflation irrelevant to wage settlements while protecting workers against subsequent inflation. This objective suggests that indexed contracts should incorporate two provisions: (1) a pay settlement should be based solely on the prices ruling when the settlement is made; (2) there must be provision for making good losses due to inflation between settlements. (2) in turn can be achieved in one of two ways, or by a combination of the two.

First, the settlement could include provision for pay revisions between settlements in proportion to changes in the index. The

[1] For a more detailed treatment of the indexation of mortgages, J. D. Whitley, 'Index-Linked Mortgages', in Liesner and King, *op. cit.*

extent to which such a provision protects workers would depend on the intervals between revisions and on the rate of inflation; the longer the first and the higher the second, the less the protection. But these deficiencies can be remedied by introducing a second protective device, namely a provision for 'back pay'. If the 'back pay' were calculated on the basis of a constant rate of inflation, it would equal half the percentage of the change of the index over the period multiplied by the pay at the last revision.[1]

*　　　*　　　*

We have not attempted an estimate of the administrative costs that indexation might entail, over and above the administrative costs inevitably associated with inflation. It is clear that these are largely confined to additional computation rather than a general increase in administrative work. As the use of computers is already widespread, additional computations are unlikely to be excessively costly.

V. FOUR KEY ASPECTS

If widespread indexation were introduced, would there be transitional problems? How might they be dealt with? What index should be adopted? Need indexation be comprehensive? Or can the main objectives be achieved by a partial indexation of some contracts? Why is indexation not widespread by now? Is there any case for making indexation of particular contracts compulsory?

The transition

It has been argued that one of the main reasons why indexation has failed to gain widespread public support is that its proponents have ignored the dislocations of transition:

'They [the proponents of indexation] tended to emphasise the desirability of the proposal as if ". . . we had a clean sheet of paper to write upon". Too often they failed to consider explicitly how the new arrangements would affect

---

[1] A more detailed account of this arrangement is in R. A. Jackman and K. Klappholz, 'The Case for Indexing Wages and Salaries', in Liesner and King, *op. cit.*, p. 29.

existing institutions and outstanding commitments. Often missing was a comprehensive analysis of the likely distribution of the total costs of transition'.[1]

The problems of transition arise because at the time of introduction of indexation there would exist a vast number of contracts denominated in monetary terms. It would be wrong simply to index them as they stand, for they will often embody expectations of inflation, and to index them would be to allow for inflation twice over. Negotiated (unindexed) wage increases in the mid-1970s already embody expectations of inflation, and to index them would be to compensate twice over for the expected increase in prices.

One possibility would be simply to replace the unindexed contracts by indexed contracts as they terminate.[2] This solution may be unsatisfactory, first, because it means that parties to existing contracts will be unprotected from any future (unanticipated) inflation, and, second, because the value of these contracts may be affected by the introduction of indexation. The other possibility is that of re-contracting, that is, replacing existing unindexed contracts by indexed ones. The difficulty here is of reaching agreement on what indexed contract is equivalent in value to the original unindexed one.

The problem is essentially bound up with the effect of the introduction of indexation on the prices of existing unindexed assets. The fear is that if an indexed bond were introduced, holders of existing securities will attempt to switch into the indexed stock, leading to a sharp decline in the price of the unindexed stock.[3] If such a sharp decline were to occur, the introduction of indexation would inflict losses on holders of assets denominated in nominal monetary terms, precisely those whom indexation is intended to protect. However if there were no decline in the value of existing unindexed securities, their holders would suffer no loss and would be able to sell their holdings and buy indexed securities at no loss, so that indexation would not make them worse off.

[1] Yang, *op. cit.*, p. 3.

[2] This is the obvious solution for short-term contracts, such as wages and salaries.

[3] 'Moreover, it appears inevitable that the adoption of a constant purchasing power Government bond would lead to a disastrous collapse in the value of outstanding investment media'. (US Congress, Joint Committee on the Economic Report, *Monetary Policy and the Management of the Public Debt*, Part 2, 82nd Congress, 2nd Session, 1952, cited by Yang, *op. cit.*, p. 5.)

We have already discussed the effect of the existence of indexed bonds on the price of unindexed securities (IV, p. 38). Our argument was that indexation would lead to a fall in the price of unindexed securities only if it were accompanied by the expectation of a faster rate of inflation. During the transition this may not be the relevant question, for expectations of the effects of indexation could not, at this stage, be based on experience of what happens with indexation. There is a widespread belief that the introduction of indexation would be taken as an admission of defeat by the government in its battle against inflation. Whatever the intrinsic merits[1] of such a view, it is clear that, if it were held on a wide enough scale, the transition to indexation would be accompanied by sharp falls in the prices of unindexed stock.

To avoid such a contingency, the government might have to stand ready to support the prices of unindexed securities. That is, it might stand prepared to buy its debt at a price equal, say, to the average value over a period immediately before the announcement of the introduction of the indexed bond. If the inflation rate does *not* accelerate, such a support policy involves no budgetary cost.

Once an 'orderly' market is established, it will be possible for, say, pension funds to purchase indexed or unindexed securities and hence offer their policy-holders an opportunity for re-contracting, that is, for specifying an indexed rather than an unindexed pension. The relative values of these options would be determined, of course, by the relative prices of indexed and unindexed securities in the market. Similarly, a comparison of the market values of claims to indexed as against unindexed income streams would provide a 'conversion table' for nonmarketable debt (e.g. mortgages) should both parties prefer to convert the contract to indexed terms.

Thus it appears that the problem of the transition is primarily one of the effect of indexation on the expected rate of inflation. If the introduction of indexation is accompanied by a general belief that inflation would accelerate, the transition would result in sharp losses to holders of monetary assets, thus exacerbating the inequities that inflation has already brought

---

[1] The basis of the argument appears to be that if, with indexation, inflation were to inflict less suffering it would also become less unpopular politically, and that would remove the government's incentive to slow down inflation (VI, section (iii)).

about. In such circumstances, the government should support the prices of its own fixed-interest stock.

This arrangement would ensure that the introduction of indexation would not, of itself, cause losses, but it would not compensate for any losses due to previous inflation. It does not seem feasible to attempt to compensate for such earlier losses.

The choice of index

The purpose of indexation is to protect the real value of contracts against unforeseen changes in the value of money. But if this purpose is to be achieved, changes in the value of money must be measured in an appropriate manner, i.e. so as to achieve the same results as if the future course of the price level were correctly foreseen. We require an index which measures 'the value of money'.

'Value of money' index

The concept of the 'value of money' is not clear, even in pure theory.[1] In practical terms there is also the question which prices are (or can be) measured. Most price indices measure the prices of a relatively limited number of goods (e.g. the retail price index) rather than the prices of all goods and assets. If there is no ideal index, which of the price indices that are available would be best suited to an indexation scheme?

Index of 'total home costs'

The most obvious choice would be a price index of consumer goods, such as the retail price index. We argue here, first, that the adoption of a retail price index would mistake the purpose of indexation, as set out here, by confusing the objective of protecting incomes from inflation with that of guaranteeing their real purchasing power. Second, it would lead to substantial problems for firms and for government policy. We conclude that the best available index would be the index of 'total home costs' rather than, as often suggested, the retail price index.[2]

[1] A. A. Alchian and L. R. Klein, 'On A Correct Measure of Inflation', *Journal of Money, Credit and Banking*, February 1973, Part I.

[2] The index of 'total home costs' is the price index of Gross Domestic Product (GDP) at factor cost. It is calculated as the ratio of GDP at current prices to GDP at constant prices. The GDP itself is measured as the sum of consumers' expenditure, investment, government expenditure on goods and services, and exports less imports less indirect taxes and plus subsidies.

It is useful to distinguish between factors which lead to a general increase in all prices (including wages and other money incomes), which may be termed 'inflationary', and factors which lead to a change in the prices of goods relatively to money incomes, which may be termed 'relative price effects'. Indexation should be linked to price increases that are the result of inflation (in the above sense of the term) and not to price increases which are the result of relative price effects. If prices rise due to an inflationary impetus, such as an increase in aggregate monetary demand, the full adjustment of the economy requires that money wages and other incomes also rise in proportion to the increase in demand, and indexing simply assists that adjustment. But if the prices of goods rise due to some relative price effect, such as a general increase in indirect taxes or a deterioration in the terms of trade, the full adjustment of the economy requires that the general level of consumer prices rise relative to the general level of money incomes. The purpose of an indirect tax increase, for example, is to transfer resources from the personal sector to the government. Such a purpose is negated by indexing arrangements which protect personal incomes against such tax increases.

Index of retail prices

The adoption of the Index of Retail Prices could be a source of serious difficulties. We may consider, for example, the effects of a general increase in indirect taxation. This will lead to a rise in the retail price index relative to firms' selling prices before tax. If wages are linked to the retail price index, firms' wage costs will inevitably rise relative to their revenues. In general, firms will be unable to pay higher wage bills, and they may react in one of two ways. First, they may accept the higher wage bill, and consequently lower profits, in the short run, but when the wage contract comes up for re-negotiation reduce any wage increase they are then prepared to offer by the full amount of the indexed increase. The alternative is for firms to accept a higher level of wage costs, and reduce output and employment and raise their prices.[1] To the extent that

---

[1] The increase in prices will lead to a further increase in wages, a further increase in prices and so on, but in the absence of an increase in aggregate monetary demand, these second-round increases will be small, and the process will not spiral indefinitely.

firms react in this way, output and employment in the economy will be lower and prices higher than in the absence of indexation.

There is a further consequence. In formulating their policies, governments will take into account the effects of relative price movements on the retail price index. They will be aware that, say, an increase in indirect taxes in an economy with indexed wages will lead to a reduction in output and employment and an increase in prices (over and above the immediate impact of the indirect tax). Governments will then have to judge policies not only on their intrinsic merits but also on their effects on the retail price index. This concern will encourage governments to reduce indirect taxes, increase subsidies, control prices and prop up the exchange rate purely for their effects on the price index. Similarly, such indexing arrangements would limit the extent to which governments can raise indirect taxes, etc. when thought desirable on other grounds, for fear of the effects on industry's wage costs.

These difficulties, at least, can be avoided by the adoption of the 'total home costs' index. Since this index excludes indirect taxes and import prices, it will not lead to the distortionary effects discussed above, and, since it cannot be readily influenced by government, it does not lead to the same bias in policy.

The 'total home costs' index is published quarterly. We believe it is the most appropriate measure of what is sometimes called the 'underlying rate of inflation'. It is therefore best suited to any indexation scheme in the UK.

It is sometimes suggested that indices should vary with types of contracts. If the aim of indexation is to compensate for changes in the value of money, it is clear that only a single index is required. The argument does not rule out the use of indexation for other objectives (e.g. insurance against relative price changes), which may imply different indices, but these other objectives should be clearly distinguished from the purpose of indexation, protection against the effects of changes in the value of money, as set out in this *Paper*.

It may be argued that the 'total home costs' index might be unacceptable because it does not protect people from all increases in the cost of living. But, as we have argued, it is impossible to protect everyone against increases in import prices, or indirect taxes, and to protect some can only throw a heavier burden on others. Do people who insist they would accept indexation only if the retail price index were used really believe they can be exempted from having to pay any increase in indirect taxes? We believe that the index of total home costs, presented as a measure of the underlying rate of domestic inflation, would prove generally acceptable.

Partial indexation

If indexation protects people from inflation, why is it not widespread? If it protects parties to a contract from subsequent unexpected changes in the value of money, why are contracts still drawn up in nominal monetary terms? We must admit at the outset that we have no completely satisfactory answer to this question. But, unless the government adopts indexation in its own contracts, indexation in the economy as a whole cannot be comprehensive. With comprehensive indexation, people are fully protected against the uncertainties of inflation. But this argument does not imply that partial indexation provides partial protection. On the contrary, it may result in people being more rather than less vulnerable to the uncertainties of inflation.[1]

If the tax system is not indexed, a firm may expect to face a higher real tax burden the faster the rate of inflation. If it contracts debts denominated in monetary terms, its real repayments will be lower the faster the rate of inflation. The firm can thus reduce the total risk it faces from variations in the inflation rate. It may therefore face less uncertainty if it issues unindexed rather than indexed debt.

But by issuing unindexed debt, it simply transfers the uncertainty from itself to its creditors. Unless they are less risk-averse than the firm, there seems nothing to be gained from such an arrangement. But if its creditors are amongst those who expect to gain from inflation, by accepting unindexed stock, they too could reduce the total risk they would face from variations in the inflation rate.

This provides one reason why the private sector may not have introduced indexation. If the government redistributes income between individuals by unanticipated inflation, the private sector may try to offset such redistributions by operating

[1] This is an example of 'second-best'. An arrangement which leads to a maximum of efficiency if applied throughout the economy may not necessarily lead to an improvement in efficiency if applied to only one sector.

markets in unindexed debt which allows a 'matching of risks': individuals and firms can try to balance unindexed assets against unindexed liabilities so that their net position is unaffected by inflation.

Even apart from the non-indexation of the public sector, a firm may find it difficult to introduce indexed contracts in the absence of comprehensive indexation in the private sector. A firm may, for example, be considering whether or not to introduce an indexed wage contract. If it is part of an industry where indexation of wages has not been generally introduced, the costs of other firms will rise as a result of wage settlements which will depend on the expected, rather than the actual, rate of inflation. If the price of the product reflects these costs, it will also depend on the expected, rather than the actual, rate of inflation. A firm which introduced indexation would find its wage costs rising with the actual rate of inflation, since wages are adjusted to changes in the index, while its product price was rising with the expected rate, and hence it would face more uncertainty than if it had negotiated an unindexed wage contract taking account of the expected rate of inflation.

Here we have a situation in which, if all firms in the industry were to index their wage contracts, all would be better off, but no individual firm will introduce indexing unless it expects the other firms to introduce it as well. (An analogy might be with decimal currency: all firms may now prefer decimal currency, but it is unlikely that any would have adopted it of their own volition had there been free choice.)

Yet these arguments, based on the disadvantage of partial rather than comprehensive indexation, scarcely provide an adequate explanation of the rarity of indexation, and its complete absence in capital markets. Should the reluctance of the private sector to introduce indexing be interpeted as indicating that indexing is not desirable, because, say, the administrative costs outweigh the benefits? Or are there reasons why the private sector may not have introduced indexation even though it would be beneficial? Would such reasons justify legislation to make indexation compulsory?

Is there a case for compulsory indexation?

We assume now that the tax system and other public sector contracts are indexed, and ask whether the indexation of private contracts should be made compulsory or be left to the choice of the parties involved. It has been argued that, although the law should make indexed contracts enforceable, whether or not they are introduced in the private sector should not be a matter of government policy but left to voluntary decision.[1]

On economic grounds, the argument that indexing should be left to the voluntary choice of the parties involved rests on the classic 'invisible-hand' mechanism according to which, if individuals act in their own self-interest, the result is an efficient outcome for society as a whole. The operation of this mechanism requires (amongst other things) that there are no 'external effects' of an economic transaction on third parties. In the context of indexation we would have to ask whether the effects of indexing a contract were confined to the parties to it, or extended to others as well, in which event there might be an argument for some form of government policy relating to the introduction of indexed contracts in the private sector.

We see three possible grounds for arguing a case for compulsory indexation.

(i) Indexation and capital markets

If a market is maintained in unindexed debt, it may misallocate investment funds (p. 20). If it operates in parallel with a market in indexed debt, it will attract only lenders who expect a particularly slow rate of inflation and borrowers who expect a particularly rapid rate.[2] Clearly, at least one of the parties to such unindexed contracts will be disappointed. This experience may discourage people from entering into such contracts, and the market in unindexed debt may not survive on a large scale. Nonetheless, insofar as the losses consequent upon the misallocation of funds are not wholly borne by the individuals entering into such contracts, there may be a case for a policy discouraging the market in unindexed debt.

---

[1] Friedman, *op. cit.*, p. 21; H. Genberg and A. K. Swoboda, 'Inflation and Indexation: a Survey of Issues', in *The Role of Indexation*, Proceedings of the Saltsjobaden Conference, July 1974, p. 17.

[2] It should be noted that this possibility does not depend on there being a general and systematic difference in expectations between borrowers and lenders. The likelihood of such a systematic difference of expectations seems remote, but it presumably forms the basis of Friedman's argument that 'businesses [tend] to defer capital investment once total spending begins to decline . . . in expectation of lower prices and lower interest rates'. (Friedman, *op. cit.*, p. 29.)

(ii) Indexation to neutralise inflationary expectations

We have argued (III, (iv), p. 32) that the indexation of wages would reduce the costs to society of slowing down the rate of inflation. If we assume that, with widespread indexation of wages, the government would be more likely to pursue a restrictive monetary policy to slow down the inflation (VI, (iii)), and that are duction in the rate of inflation would benefit society as a whole, the indexation of wages could be regarded as a 'public good', for the benefits of reduced inflation accrue to all members of society, and not solely to those who have introduced indexed wage contracts.

The argument here can also be set out in the following way. If wage contracts are not indexed, firms and individuals must make estimates of the future rate of inflation, which may turn out to be mistaken. Insofar as the mistakes may lead to unemployment or bankruptcies, the government may intervene by resorting to expansionary monetary policy, which essentially shifts the costs of the mistaken estimates from those who made them to the community as a whole through a higher rate of inflation. This reduces the costs to individuals of their mistaken estimates. If they expect the government to bail them out whenever they make wrong estimates, the incentive to avoid wrong estimates is correspondingly reduced. Indexed wage contracts are one means whereby such wrong estimates can be avoided, for with indexing it is unnecessary to make any estimates of the future rate of inflation. Thus the incentive to introduce indexation is weakened.

(iii) Indexation and money illusion

Will those who benefit from inflation refuse to accept indexed contracts which would put an end to such benefits? If both parties to the contract have the same expectations about the future rate of inflation, indexation is to the advantage of both. The contract would embody the expected rate of inflation, and the absence of indexation would simply mean increased uncertainty for both parties.

But if the parties to the contract have different expectations about inflation, unindexed contracts can be used by individuals and private sector institutions, as well as by governments, as a means of improving their position. For example, if trade union leaders (and employers) expect a faster rate of inflation than do trade union members, the leaders will appear to achieve larger real wage increases for their members in times of inflation than in times of price stability. This result might be expected to strengthen the position of the leaders relative to their members, as long as the differential expectations persist. Indexation would remove the opportunities for such gains by trade union leaders, and hence may be opposed by them.

Similarly, private sector financial institutions may be able to benefit at the expense of savers, if the latter expect a lower rate of inflation. They may also be opposed to the introduction of indexation.

These redistributions serve no purpose in terms of economic efficiency (p. 17); hence indexation, which would prevent such redistributions, cannot be regarded as undesirable on these grounds. Yet these considerations provide an incentive for private sector institutions to oppose the introduction of indexation.

To summarise, there may be a case for compulsory indexation in capital markets to protect the ignorant and economically unsophisticated. There may be a case for compulsory indexation of wages to be accompanied by deflationary monetary policies as a means of minimising the unemployment costs of slowing down inflation. These arguments do not necessarily provide a conclusive case for compulsion, but indicate the reasons for which it might be justified.

VI. INDEXATION, POLITICS AND ECONOMIC POLICY

We have argued that indexation would largely eliminate the effects of uncertainty about the future course of the price level, prevent the redistributions which result from (unanticipated) inflation, and mitigate some of its inefficiencies. If inflation continued with indexation, the effects would be those of *correctly anticipated* inflation, whose inefficiencies indexation would not remedy. The case for indexation therefore rests on the view that unanticipated inflation or deflation is likely from time to time.[1]

We now consider:

(i) whether there are good reasons for expecting continued fluctuations in the rate of inflation, the contingency which provides the *rationale* of proposals for indexation;

(ii) whether inflation would matter in the presence of indexation;

(iii) how indexation might affect the rate of inflation;

(iv) whether indexation might not cause difficulties in achieving other aims of macro-economic policy particularly relevant at the present time.

(i) *Would the inflation rate continue to fluctuate in the absence of indexation?*

The answer to this question depends on what determines the rate of inflation. If the 'cost-push' mechanism, discussed in III, (iii), is at work, inflation results from the incompatible demands of the participants in the productive process, which would seem to depend on sociological factors about which little is known.

If inflation is explained by the demand-expectations theory, the answer to our question depends, in addition, on the likely course of government economic policies.

The government can derive some 'benefit' from a constant positive rate of inflation, namely the inflation tax on currency holdings and, if there are political constraints on raising real tax rates explicitly, the additional real revenue which may accrue with inflation (III, (i)). Some of the major political 'benefits' accrue from unanticipated inflation, namely, the employment effects and the redistributive effects from changes in the real value of the National Debt. According to the demand-expectations theory, however, these effects do not outlast the public realisation that the rate of inflation has increased.

---

[1] 'The case for indexation, . . . is essentially based on the judgement that anticipations about price level changes are neither uniform nor very accurate'. (Yang, *op. cit.*, p. 10.) Even if, on average, we could expect a constant rate of inflation, there would still be fluctuations in its rate which, as we have argued, fulfil no necessary economic functions and have effects which are generally regarded as undesirable. Hence, economists made various proposals for indexation long before the spectre of inflation stalked the world. (Brian Griffiths, 'English Classical Political Economy and the Debate on Indexation', in Friedman, *op. cit.*, pp. 39-45, and M. Friedman, 'Inflation, Taxation and Indexation', a discussion in *Inflation: Causes, Consequences, Cures*, IEA Readings No. 14, 1974, pp. 81-2.)

Beyond this stage, the attempt to maintain the 'benefits' of the higher employment level and lower real interest rates would require constantly *accelerating* inflation. This outcome would be regarded as politically unacceptable, so the policies which led to the acceleration of inflation would be modified, resulting in fluctuating inflation rates. Thus, the demand-expectations theory of inflation combined with uncontroversial views about the political incentives facing present-day governments suggest that it is not fanciful to expect fluctuating inflation rates, i.e. the contingency on which the case for indexation rests.[1]

(ii) With indexation, would inflation matter?

Indexation would largely neutralise the effects of inflation, and of fluctuations in its rate. It may therefore be asked whether indexation would make the general level of prices a matter of complete indifference. Since, according to most proposals for indexation, currency would not be indexed, the answer is clearly 'No', as people could sustain gains and losses on their currency holdings (II, (ii)). This answer, however, only invites the further question, 'Why not index currency?' A partial reply is that it would be extremely costly to index currency (as individuals would have to provide evidence about how long they had held a particular note!).

A more fundamental, if perhaps paradoxical, reply is that even if currency were indexed, the price level would not be a matter of indifference. This is the main argument against indexing currency. The reason why the price level would matter is simply that money would continue to be used as a unit of account, so that prices would be quoted in terms of units of money. The more unstable the price level, the more often prices have to be changed. Frequent changes in prices—induced by the instability of the price level—impose significant costs and inconveniences without offsetting benefits. It would be otiose to try to support this contention with detailed argument at a time when, for example, postal rates will have changed

[1] The demand-expectations theory is not to be confused with the original Phillips Curve theory, according to which alternative *constant* inflation rates were associated with different levels of employment. Sometimes indexation was recommended on the basis of the original Phillips Curve theory (e.g., M. J. Farrell, *Fuller Employment?*, Hobart Paper 34, IEA, 1965). Since this involved choosing between alternative steady inflation rates, it offered no strong arguments for indexation. However both theoretical criticism and recent economic history have dealt heavy blows to the original Phillips Curve theory.

twice in one year and the Post Office cannot produce books of stamps to keep pace with these changes. It is therefore quite logical to wish to introduce indexation partly to help slow down inflation.

Indexation of currency would validate any accidental change in the price level by the resulting change in the amount of currency outstanding. There would be no 'equilibrium price level'; instead, the price level could be anything.[1] It is plausible to suppose that, in such circumstances, the price level could rise or fall without limit. Given that the price level *would* matter even with indexation, these considerations provide powerful arguments against indexing currency, quite apart from the practical difficulties.

Opponents of indexation would regard the above remarks about the costs of variability in the price level as a powerful concession to their case, on the ground that indexation can be expected to lead to more inflation. Even if it did so, that clearly could not by itself be a conclusive argument against it, if some of its benefits are acknowledged. But it is therefore important to consider how indexation might affect the behaviour of the price level.

(iii) *Indexation and the behaviour of the price level*

We accept the view that, except in the very short term, the behaviour of the price level depends largely on the growth of the money supply. The question therefore is whether there are reasons to suppose that the growth of the money supply would be affected by indexation. Whether or not governments acknowledge that they control the growth of the money supply, the truth remains that they do. The question then becomes whether the prevalence of indexation would induce governments to pursue different policies on monetary growth than they otherwise do. Unfortunately, general considerations yield no clear answer to this question.

We may assume that, with or without indexation, governments weigh the political costs and benefits (to themselves!) of pursuing inflationary policies. Governments presumably gain politically by raising the level of employment, and lose politically from the concomitant acceleration of inflation. With indexation, the political costs of (a given) increase in the inflation rate would presumably fall, and for this reason one

[1] Genberg and Swoboda, *op. cit.*, p. 12, for further discussion.

might expect governments to opt for a *higher* inflation rate. On the other hand, the political benefits (in increased employment and additional government revenue) of a given increase in the inflation rate would be smaller with indexation (III) and for that reason one would expect the government to opt for a *lower* inflation rate. Since the two effects go in opposite directions, the net effect depends on their relative magnitudes. These general arguments leave open the question of the effect of indexation on the average rate of inflation.[1]

A frequently heard argument is that indexation would permanently raise the inflation rate because it would be taken as a sign that the government had given up the fight against inflation. Such expectations could not be permanently self-fulfilling, since a permanently higher inflation rate would require a permanently faster growth in the money supply. Friedman mentions an argument to suggest that the money supply would grow faster with indexation.[2] With full indexation of taxes and government debt, the inflation tax would be confined to the tax on currency holdings. If the government wished to obtain a *given* amount of revenue from inflation (as distinct from maximising its political net benefits) the inflation rate would have to rise. This argument does not answer the question why a government should seek a given amount of revenue from a given tax, rather than maximise the net benefits it derives from its policies.

(iv) *Indexation and some current issues of policy*

Readers may accept the arguments that we are likely to face conditions which make the distributive and efficiency effects of indexation desirable and also that general arguments yield no prediction about the effect of indexation on the rate of inflation. They may still have misgivings about introducing indexation in the UK at the present time, when the country is 'living beyond its means' and when most commentators are agreed that 'retrenchment' is required. Would indexation not make retrenchment more difficult if not impossible? Although these misgivings are usually not formulated explicitly, we believe they are behind some of the objections to indexation. We shall try to make these possible objections explicit and to answer

---

[1] For further, and equally inconclusive arguments, Genberg and Swoboda, *op. cit.*, pp. 12-13.

[2] *Op. cit.*, p. 31.

them. In doing so we shall be drawing on arguments developed earlier.

One area of retrenchment concerns the balance of payments. The reduction or elimination of the current account deficit requires a rise in the value of exports relative to the value of imports.

(a) One way of achieving this result is by permitting a further depreciation of sterling. This would raise the price of exports and imports in terms of domestic currency, encourage exports by making them more profitable, and reduce imports. As a consequence real home incomes would fall, since the price of imports will have risen relatively to home money incomes. If home money incomes now rose to offset the rise in import prices, the effect of the depreciation would be nullified. It may be feared that indexation would have precisely this effect. This fear is unjustified if indexation is linked to an index which excludes the effects of changes in import prices relatively to home money incomes (V, (ii)).[1]

It is often argued that, even in the absence of indexation, initial increases in import prices would be neutralised by subsequent increases in domestic money wages and prices, because workers would refuse to accept reductions in real incomes. For this reason the imposition of import controls is sometimes recommended to improve the balance of trade without further depreciation. This argument is part of the 'cost-push' theory examined in III, insofar as it supposes that workers have 'non-negotiable' demands for real income.[2]

[1] It appears that indexation in Finland 'was brought to an end in 1968 after the devaluation of the Markaa. It was felt that comprehensive linking of financial assets and wages . . . mitigated a fall in real wages and reduced the favourable effect of the parity change'. (*The Role of Indexation*, Proceedings of the Saltsjobaden Conference, 4-6 July, 1974, International Center for Monetary and Banking Studies, Geneva, p. 23). It must be noted that in Finland indexation was *not* based on an index which excluded the effects of changes in import prices relatively to home money incomes.

It is, incidentally, surprising to find a 'monetarist' claiming that devaluation 'accounts' for (part of) domestic inflation. (R. Harris, ' "A Self-confessed Monetarist" . . .?' in *British Economic Policy 1970-74*, Hobart Paperback No. 7, IEA, 1975, p. 13, note 2.

[2] *Economic Policy Review*, February 1975, Department of Applied Economics, University of Cambridge. The advocates of import controls seem unaware of an elementary proposition of economic analysis, namely that import controls impose larger rather than smaller real income costs than a depreciation of the currency in achieving a given balance-of-payments improvement. (W. M. Corden, I. M. D. Little and M. FG. Scott, *Import Controls versus Devaluation and Britain's Economic Prospects*, Trade Policy Research Centre, March 1975.)

(*b*) Another means of improving the balance of payments is a reduction in demand and employment. The indexation of wages may make the level of employment less sensitive to government policy (III, (iv)). It might therefore be argued that indexation would have the undesirable effect of weakening the government's ability to correct the balance of payments by demand management policies.

In reply to this objection, it is necessary to distinguish between two situations. If the balance-of-payments deficit is a consequence of domestic 'over-full employment', then demand-reducing policies are indeed the appropriate remedy. But, as argued in III, (iv), indexation would make it more difficult to create conditions of 'over-full employment' in the first place.

If, on the other hand, there is a balance-of-payments deficit at a time of less than full employment, the appropriate remedy is not further deflation, but a reduction in domestic prices relatively to world prices. Indexation may reduce the government's ability to create additional unemployment in these circumstances, but in so doing it only weakens what is in any event an undesirable policy. The appropriate policy, a reduction in relative prices, may be achieved by a depreciation of the exchange rate ((*a*) above) or by a reduction in domestic prices. The latter may be more easily achieved with indexation (III (iv)).

(*c*) This brings us to the question whether indexation would affect the functioning of alternative possible exchange-rate régimes: rigidly fixed exchange rates, some kind of adjustable peg, and freely floating, or managed, exchange rates.

Rigidly fixed exchange rates will become agenda for policy if the EEC moves towards monetary union. The adoption of fixed exchange rates among a group of countries does not necessarily imply a commitment to price stability, but does imply a commitment to maintain the same inflation rates which may, of course, fluctuate. Rigidly fixed exchange rates thus do not rule out the contingency on which the case for indexation rests, nor would their functioning be affected by indexation.

It could be argued that indexation might have different effects on inflation rates in the various countries, thus making the maintenance of fixed rates impossible. But fixed rates are maintainable only if there is a mechanism to ensure that rates of growth of the money supply in these countries keep in step. Given such a mechanism, indexation would not affect the functioning of fixed rates, and without it fixed rates cannot be maintained.

If a country has pegged rates, but a higher inflation rate than its trading partners, it will sooner or later have to devalue, while with floating rates the depreciation would occur more smoothly. Since in either case the index we propose would exclude the effects of changing import prices, we can see no connection between indexation and the feasibility of different exchange-rate régimes.

(*d*) Do the UK's heavy foreign debts introduce a complication? If foreigners held indexed assets in this country, it might be feared that there would be an additional 'burden' on the balance of payments. It is, of course, true that indexation would protect foreigners against unanticipated inflation, just as it would protect domestic residents. It is in any event more difficult to expropriate foreigners through inflation than domestic residents, since in the UK foreigners, unlike residents, have the right to move their assets abroad freely. In the present context, indexation would have the merit of putting domestic residents on a footing of equality with foreigners.

(*e*) Finally, it is popularly believed that the slowing down of inflation itself requires 'sacrifices' in real living standards. It is indeed the desire to share such sacrifices more fairly that motivated the 'flat-rate' £6 a week incomes policy introduced in August 1975.[1] Would indexation prevent this sacrifice in living standards?

The reduction in living standards is presumably necessary because a deceleration in the rate of inflation is typically accompanied by a rise in unemployment, thus reducing real output. We must first note, therefore, that indexation would of itself reduce the need for such a sacrifice insofar as it would reduce the unemployment costs of slowing down inflation (III, (iv)). With indexation, there would be less of a sacrifice to share, and hence less justification for distortionary policies proposed to make the sacrifice more 'acceptable'.

Even so, real incomes may have to be reduced, and the fear is expressed that indexation would make this reduction impossible. The argument is, presumably, that, with indexation, real incomes before tax cannot be reduced by inflation. But this process would not in any event reduce demand (III, (ii)).

[1] *The Attack on Inflation*, Cmnd. 6151, HMSO, July 1975.

What is required is a reduction in real incomes after tax. It may then be argued that some policies to reduce real incomes after tax, e.g. increases in indirect taxes or reductions in subsidies, may themselves be nullified by indexation.

If indexation were based on an index which included the effects of changes in indirect taxes and subsidies, such as the Index of Retail Prices, indexation would indeed cause difficulties for such policies (V, p. 47). These difficulties could be avoided by basing indexation on the index of total home costs. It must be emphasised again that, if indexation is related to an appropriately defined price index, it does not offer 'protection' to individuals against changes in real tax rates or prevent the government from acquiring more revenue from any given real national income.

CONCLUSION

We conclude that, with or without indexing, the inflation rate will continue to fluctuate. In these circumstances, widespread indexation would be a substantial benefit. It is sometimes suggested, both by economists and by politicians, that indexation is an alternative to price stability. Genberg and Swoboda argue that:

> 'the best policy remains the control and eradication of inflation itself. If indexation can help us live with inflation, stopping inflation can help us live without indexation'.[1]

But indexation and price stability are not alternative policies; we could have both, just as we may carry umbrellas in fine weather.

The quotation suggests a more fundamental question about the political feasibility of introducing indexation. Since indexation would neutralise most of the effects of inflation, why should it be politically easier to introduce indexation than to stop inflation?[2] If there are groups who gain from inflation and who have the political power to induce governments to pursue inflationary policies, would they not also have the power to prevent the introduction of indexation? We cannot pretend to have convincing answers to this question, and have to content ourselves with general observations.

[1] *The Role of Indexation*, p. 22. Cf. M. Friedman, *op. cit.*, p. 20.

[2] This question is different from that of the effect of indexation on the rate of inflation, which was considered in section (iii) (above, p. 56), for there we took indexation as given.

The gains from inflation are gains from unanticipated inflation. If those who benefit from inflation have the political power, and are prepared to see runaway inflation, the introduction of indexation might well be impossible.

But if the balance of political power is not such as to lead to runaway inflation, at some point government will prevetn further acceleration of inflation, and this will lead to an erosion of the benefits of inflation to the groups that induced the inflationary policies. At this stage, inflation may be of no benefit to anyone, yet there is a substantial cost in unemployment of slowing it down. If indexation can reduce this cost, it might well be acceptable.

This picture assumes that those involved are unaware of the long-term consequences of their behaviour. If it is supposed that, when policies are considered, their consequences are always perfectly understood, there would be no further scope for rational argument about them. We believe, on the contrary, that misunderstandings are widespread about the consequences of economic policies, including the consequences of indexation. The more these misunderstandings can be removed, the less excuse will governments have for not introducing indexation.

Governments continually claim to be appalled by the consequences of inflation, for which they also refuse to accept responsibility. We do not accept the view that persistent inflation can take place regardless of government policy. But even if governments are not prepared to stop inflation, indexation would largely protect citizens from its effects. It therefore must be emphasised that indexation offers governments the means to protect their citizens against inflation. If governments refuse to employ this means, then at best they must be judged ill-informed, and at worst the integrity of their protestations must be questioned.

QUESTIONS FOR DISCUSSION

1. What is the difference, in terms of resource allocation and income distribution, between a fully indexed economy with a fluctuating price level and an unindexed economy with a constant price level? Which would you regard as preferable? Which do you think would be more likely to come about? Explain.

2. It is argued that indexation protects people from inflation. Would it not be a good idea also to protect people from the consequences of, say, technological progress, a change in fashion, an increase in import prices, or a change in government taxation policy? What arrangements might be made for such purposes, and what problems might arise?

3. In an inflation, people desire to hold more real and fewer financial assets than in times of price stability. How might this lead to a loss of economic efficiency? Would such losses be avoided by indexation?

4. 'If all contracts were indexed, and an inflation were to start, there would be nothing to stop it.' Do you agree?

5. Outline the 'cost-push' model of inflation. If this were an accurate representation of the inflationary process, what would be the effect of introducing indexation?

6. In times of rapid inflation, nominal interest rates often fall below the rate of inflation, so that real interest rates become negative. Why do you think this happens? What would you expect to happen to real interest rates in an indexed economy?

7. If indexation protects people from unanticipated changes in the value of money subsequent to the signing of contracts, why are indexed contracts not already widespread in the private sector?

8. 'For the government, I propose that escalator clauses [indexation] be legislated; for the rest of the economy, that they be voluntary, but that any legal obstacles be removed' (Milton Friedman). In what circumstances might Friedman's proposal be regarded as inadequate?

9. People might regard the introduction of indexation as a sign that the government had given up the fight against inflation. Critically examine this viewpoint.

[63]

10. 'Statutory indexation is no different from a statutory incomes policy, and suffers from all the same problems.' Do you agree?

11. 'It is absurd to introduce indexation, which would ensure that living standards are maintained, at a time when "the nation is living beyond its means", and real living standards must be reduced.' Discuss.

12. 'Indexation means that real wages are fixed, and hence that the level of unemployment is independent of the level of aggregate demand. Thus it radically transforms our approach to macro-economic policy.' Discuss.

BIBLIOGRAPHY

A comprehensive historical bibliography of works on indexation is provided by Brian Griffiths in Milton Friedman, *Monetary Correction*, IEA Occasional Paper No. 41. Amongst recent work, important contributions are:

Alchian, A. A., and Klein, L. R., 'On A Correct Measure of Inflation', *Journal of Money, Credit and Banking*, February 1973, Part I.

American Enterprise Institute, *Essays on Inflation and Indexation*, Domestic Affairs Studies No. 24, Washington, DC, 1974.

Fischer, S., 'The Demand for Index Bonds', *Journal of Political Economy*, June 1975.

Friedman, Milton, *Monetary Correction*, Occasional Paper 41, Institute of Economic Affairs, 1974.

Liesner, Thelma, and King, M., (eds.), *Indexing for Inflation*, Institute for Fiscal Studies, 1975.

National Institute of Economic and Social Research, *National Institute Economic Review*, November 1974.

Robson, P., 'Inflation-Proof Loans', *National Westminster Bank Quarterly Review*, May 1974.

Swoboda, A. K., and Genberg, H., (eds.), *The Role of Indexation*, Proceedings of the Saltsjobaden Conference, July 1974.

Yang, J-H., 'The Case For and Against Indexation: An Attempt at Perspective', *Federal Reserve Bank of St. Louis Review*, October 1974.